GROW OR DIE

Books by David The Good

General Gardening
Start a Home-Based Plant Nursery

Florida Gardening
Totally Crazy Easy Florida Gardening
Create Your Own Florida Food Forest
Florida Survival Gardening

The Good Guides
Compost Everything
Grow or Die
Push the Zone
Free Plants for Everyone

Jack Broccoli Novels
Turned Earth
Garden Heat

GROW OR DIE

The Good Guide to Survival Gardening

David The Good

Grow or Die
David The Good

Copyright © 2021 by David The Good.

Cover by Andrew Chandler

Good Books Publishing
goodbookspub.com

ISBN: 978-1-955289-00-9

Contents

Introduction

There's something strange going on right now.

The world has been turned upside-down. Trillions are being printed. The pandemic caused shortages in everything from toilet paper to lumber.

Politicians have failed us and justice seems to be dead.

People who used to hate guns are now buying ARs and truckloads of ammo.

Folks who never saved a dime are buying silver dollars.

Canned beans and bags of rice are getting stuffed under mattresses.

And gardening... is no longer a hobby.

The zeitgeist has shifted from prosperous optimism to a pervasive unease mixed with distrust and outright fear.

If you're ready to quit worrying about the future and pull up your fears by the roots, you need to start gardening. You need to know how to feed yourself should the doomsayers be correct. In good times it's easy to outsource your food production to thousands of miles away... in bad times, relying on far-off farmers and tenuous shipping conduits is worse than foolish.

I'm not a brilliant investor or prognosticator. I'm not a tactical guru or a doomsday prepper. I am, however, a really good gardener who grows almost all of his family's vegetables and a sizable portion of their roots and fruits. If you've read my book *Compost Everything: The Good Guide to Extreme Composting*, you also know that I'm willing to try and test almost anything to see if it works.

The gardening advice you're going to read in this book is based on my own research and on years of tweaking methods in order to get the most food for the least amount of work. When things get ugly, you don't want to rely on books written for hobby gardeners or the advice of folks who are interested in selling fancy tools, fertilizers, and overpriced hybrid vegetables starts at the local garden center. I've killed more plants than most people have ever grown. If there's a gardening problem, I've probably encountered it and slapped it silly.

Yeah, I'm totally bragging.

My desire is for you to feel the same way I do: confident in your ability to grow what you and your family will need to survive no matter what the future holds. I want you to view your hoe the way a soldier views his rifle—as insurance against whatever comes around the next corner.

Despite claims to the contrary, we are not short on land.

We are, however, short on land that is being used for food production.

A lot of crummy suburbs of over-inflated vinyl-clad houses were built on what was once prime farmland. Worthless grass now covers good soil that could easily be pressed back into use in an emergency.

Your yard may be one of those patches of worthless grass—but if things get ugly, that grass will have to go.

Let's picture a scenario.

Imagine a nuke goes off in the Middle East, causing the price of oil to soar. Because of the resulting explosion in gas prices, trucks are no longer transporting food and supplies as far across the country, and local grocery stores are rapidly emptied in a panic.

Most Americans (with the exception of Mormons and preppers) have very little food stored up for an emergency. Those that do have food stored up often don't have enough.

And besides, the idea of storing food, rather than growing it, is much like living off your savings account and not getting a job. Eventually you're going to run out.

Within a few weeks of a crisis event that shuts down the food supply chain, a lot of people are going to be very hungry. Squirrels and deer will disappear from the woods, followed by raccoons, tortoises, armadillos, and anything else remotely edible.

Those that do not convert their grass into food plots are going to be in trouble.

In this book I will show you how to convert a typical yard into a food-producing machine using only simple hand tools and homemade fertilizers. It's not going to be easy, but you can grow enough to stave off starvation. You need to start now, however, rather than waiting for things to crash before you start gardening. Experimentation and preparation are key.

If you're ready to plant a garden that will get you through tough times while feeding you better produce than anything you can buy, this book is for you.

Read this book, then build on what I've already discovered. Just don't wait to start gardening. Start right now before it's too late.

Chapter 1

Methods

There is an endless search for the easiest way to garden. The fool-proof method. The no-work approach. The incredibly productive strategy.

Here's a sample of ideas you may have encountered:

- Self-watering Earthboxes
- Tower Gardens
- Plastic bottle hydroponics
- Gutter gardening
- Trash-can potatoes
- PVC pipe gardening
- Straw bale gardening
- Gardening in bags of soil
- Olla pot irrigation
- 4-season greenhouse gardening
- Strawberry barrel gardening
- Drip-line irrigated rows

...and lots more.

Now I'm not going to condemn all these methods. Many of them are quite clever and may be perfect for your area, particularly if you're in a marginal food growing area. My main problem with most of these methods is that in a grid-down situation, or in a post peak oil scenario, or even during a time of runaway inflation or a shipping strike of some sort, you may get stuck.

A lot of these methods purport to be easy short-cuts to growing your own food. The concern is, however, that the methods are too complex or driven by outside inputs to work well in a crisis. The ideal survival garden is a dead-simple garden.

Before I go further, let me say this: if you're growing your own food, however you're doing it, you're better off than the many people who aren't growing anything at all. If it takes an irrigation system divided into carefully timed sectors and automatic sprinklers to keep you producing edibles, that's a lot better than doing nothing.

That caveat aside, I have some worries. Let's pretend you're on city water and electricity. Let's further pretend that you've set up the coolest danged tilapia-raising/cabbage-growing/self-filtering aquaponics system this side of Star Trek. What do you do if the power goes off... or your access to easy water dries up?

This isn't a hypothetical question. I have a friend who raises tilapia and salads in a greenhouse. It's cool as heck and totally worth seeing. Yet on two separate occasions, he's lost a bunch of his fish because of minor flaws he didn't catch until it was too late. At one point his aeration valve locked up while his pump continued to empty water from the system. A tank drained overnight, and by the time he saw it the next morning, he had a bunch of dead fish.

This is sad but not life-threatening right now. But if those fish were needed to feed the family because there were no other options left, he would have been in big trouble. Sometimes one little problem can really mess up a complicated system.

Part of the reason our nation is in such trouble is because the American banking system and the international banking system—aided by bought-and-sold governments—kept bundling, repackaging, leveraging, and building vast castles of wealth on top of a shaky and increasingly incomprehensible system of debt-backed paper money. In gardening terms, they moved far away from the simplicities of dirt, sunlight, digging, and seeding... and the resulting crash in '08 created a mess which was papered over with even more debt, ensuring that the next crash will be even worse.

My advice to new gardeners and those who hope to feed themselves through future cataclysms is the same thing I learned when I was an editor for my college's newspaper: KISS. That's short for Keep It Simple, Stupid!

You may be facing tough conditions on your property. Perhaps the soil is too alkaline or comprised of hard clay, or, heaven forbid, you're in the city and have a shady lot thanks to your neighbor's trees.

The temptation is to look for an easier way but sometimes you can't have ease and security at the same time. If a squirrel chewed through your irrigation hoses, would you be able to replace them? If a hurricane knocked down your greenhouse, could you still grow? If the power went off, would your well work?

Some of the methods above are pretty simple. The difficulties arise in doing them on a large enough scale to feed yourself.

A few generations back, gardening required skill and hard work but little in the way of infrastructure. If you stayed in shape, owned some good tools, and consistently added manure and built up your soil, you could grow food almost anywhere. You might not have been able to pull off touchy gourmet plants, but chances were there was a staple you could grow that would keep you from getting too hungry.

Figure out how to grow with the simplest methods possible. Once you figure out how to garden traditionally, there's no reason not to fiddle around with more complicated approaches as they tickle your fancy. Redundancy is always a good idea. In my gardening, I maintain a range of different approaches and always plant a variety of staples, from easy roots like turnips to long-term food sources like chestnuts and other tree crops.

Preparedness should start from the ground up. Get good at doing things simply, and you can always add complexity later. Just don't count on those systems for everything.

Now let's take a look at some common (and generally simple) gardening methods and their pros and cons.

Raised Beds

Most modern gardening books embrace the raised bed as if it were the greatest invention since the Scots created peat-flavored alcohol.

Raised beds are the modern way to garden. The good way. The BEST way!

Let me count the ways they're amazing:

1. Raised beds give you good boundaries.
2. Raised beds help the soil warm up quicker in the spring.
3. Raised beds make for good drainage.
4. Raised beds work well for intensive plantings.
5. Raised beds allow you to garden in nicer dirt than your native soil.

I think that's about it. I probably missed one or ten, but who cares. We know what we need to know: RAISED BEDS ARE AWESOME!!!

Actually, I'm not so sure about that anymore. Raised beds have their uses, but they're not the gardening end-all. In fact, I think they may be holding us back from doing even better.

Let's look at some problems with raised beds.

Drainage

Having beds that drain well is a plus, right? Well, it depends on your local weather. One of the difficulties in being an internationally published garden writer is that it's difficult to give solid gardening advice for every climate. In places with wet springs, having good drainage is a plus. You don't want your seedlings rotting in cold, mucky soil. Therefore, it makes sense to raise the ground inside the bed so the soil dries out quicker.

In Florida, however, gardeners face dry springs and hot, wet summers. We also have sandy well-draining soil through much of the state. Spring is our prime gardening season, and raised beds are a pain in the neck to keep watered. The high drainage isn't an asset; it's a liability.

In the arid Southwest, gardeners will plant in sunken beds so they can gather and keep as much moisture as possible. Most gardening books that tout raised bed gardening don't take into consideration the varying climates that might not benefit from the extra drainage.

If you have fast-draining soil, skip the raised beds. They won't help.

Construction Cost and Toxicity

Unlike gardening right in the ground, it takes money and time to create most raised beds. Yes, you can make mounded raised beds by loosening the earth and raking it into mounds without borders—which works well. But most gardeners aren't doing that. Instead, they're building beds with borders.

I've built beds with pine, logs, railroad ties, tires, cinder blocks, bottles, rocks, bricks, and pressure-treated lumber.

I've never built any beds from cedar because of the prohibitive cost, but I've seen some really nice ones and thought about it. My family and I even did one bed with reclaimed mosaiced blocks. It looks really cool.

The problem is that these things cost you.

The materials cost money unless you find reclaimed materials you can salvage. In that case, the time spent building the beds still costs you.

Another thing that may cost you: many of the building materials available are at least minimally toxic. Tires can leach out poisons, cinderblocks may be made from toxic ash, pressure treated lumber is iffy, and railroad ties are nasty.

Ah well. If I had a million dollars I'd buy some cedar.

The point is, constructing raised beds with borders for a survival garden consumes time and resources that are not necessary. Your crops don't care if it looks pretty.

Dirt

Here's another reason people like raised beds: it gets them away from using their native soil. Most gardeners wish they had something else in their yards other than what they have. The ideal soil is probably volcanic loam, but most folks aren't lucky enough to have anything like that, so they decide their soil is "bad," and they decide to replace it.

Many gardeners will just buy a big pile of top soil or municipal compost or something else to plant their vegetables in. The problem with bringing in soil is that you're not exactly sure what you're bringing in. Purchased compost may be contaminated with heavy metals or toxic long-term herbicides. Some purchased "top soil" is really dead stuff, and sometimes it's just a mix of half-rotted ground-up wood chips and sand.

Your local soil often contains a wide variety of minerals, even if it's not pretty. Add some organic matter to loosen it up; throw in some seaweed, manure (if you use horse manure, compost it well first - the weeds can be insane!), epsom salt, etc., and use what you have. It's cheaper and will usually prove itself worthwhile.

Undesirable Permanence

One other thing I don't like about raised beds: their permanence.

I know, that might sound ridiculous coming from a guy that grows his own fruit trees from seed, yet I like to move my gardens around on a regular basis. I can't tell you how many times I've disassembled raised beds and moved them so I could try something new.

Having a big plot of bed-free earth is a nice thing. I can let paths evolve and then change them. I can plant a big mess of pumpkins one year, and tight beds of greens the next. Having permanent beds holds me down.

You may be the opposite, however. There's nothing really wrong with making permanent beds. I have some - I just don't do all my gardens that way.

Finally: gardening isn't a one-size-fits-all practice. There are good things about raised beds, and there are problems with raised beds—just like almost everything else in life.

If raised beds work wonderfully for you, keep using them. Just don't let yourself think they're the very best in all circumstances. Leave that view to the broad-brush garden writers and seek success wherever it can be found—inside the bed or out.

Enough about raised beds. Let's get into tilling.

Tilling

Tilling is demonized for a variety of reasons, but is it evil? If not, in what circumstances is it appropriate?

Emotions run high when tilling is mentioned. On the one side you'll find the "traditional" gardener rototilling his row garden in the spring, or the farmer with the big acreage outside town. On the other side, you'll find everyone from that hippie down the street to Paul Gautschi in the *Back to Eden* film.

It's evident that tilling the ground works well for vegetable gardening. John Jeavons's method of double-dug biointensive gardening is a form of hand tilling. Steve Solomon also endorses digging. And Dick Raymond, author of *The Joy of Gardening* loves, loves, loves his Troybilt tiller. (Of course, he also helped design it and was paid to endorse it.)

The problem is that there is no single correct way to garden. There is no fifth element capable of joining together all our gardening knowledge into one Unified Field Theory of Vegetative Nirvana.

There is you. Your land. Your tools. Seeds, sunshine, water, and nutrients, all operating in a vastly complicated ecosystem, much of which is imperceptible due to its minute size.

It makes you want to tear off your clothes and throw yourself on your knees in the mud, screaming up at the broken skies through a torrent of rain, searching for meaning in all the pain and emptiness of unknowing, doesn't it?

All right, maybe that's just me.

Tilling is one of those gray areas. There are good reasons to do it and good reasons not to. Let's look at the bad reasons first, and then the good ones.

Why Tilling Is Bad

The soil is filled with a vast web of interrelating organisms. This is called "Icky."

Just kidding. It's called "the vast web of interrelating organisms."

Tilling disrupts and inverts the soil. It tears apart the delicate fungal strands running through the ground, both buries and unearths bacteria, and wreaks havoc on the structure of vulnerable soils. Beyond that, it can create a hardpan under some circumstances. This means that below the nice fluffy part, you've compacted the layer below, sometimes to such an extent that roots cannot reach down deep for water and nutrients. Even worse, if you till around growing plants to get rid of weeds, you can do a lot of damage to their roots.

Another problem: Nature is modest and rarely appears unclad in a healthy ecosystem. She clothes herself with plants, grasses, moss and trees... drapes her form in falling autumn leaves... and wraps her curves in the soft debris and mycelium of the forest floor.

Bare soil is anathema. The ecosystem was also created to hoard seeds, which germinate under times of stress.

When you till, you turn up thousands of seeds that have been lying stored in the soil's "seed bank." If you don't start your crops quickly, the ground you tilled will rapidly be covered in new growth. If the soil is rich, you might see nettles. If you live in a hot humid climate with sandy soils, you might end up with shepherd's needle. If the soil is poor, you might get some nitrogen fixers like black medic or clover. And if the soil is compacted, you could get deep-rooted plants like chicory, dandelions, or thistle. These plants arrive to "fix" the damage the tiller has done and move the ecosystem forward to a higher level of complexity. No-till gardeners will brag about their deep mulches and how they "barely have to weed." That's because without soil disruption and inversion, most seeds simply remain dormant beneath the ground rather than growing between your tomatoes. If you till and keep the ground bare between your plants, you'll have to keep on hoeing throughout the growing season, or you'll suffer reduced or nonexistent yields.

There's no doubt about it: tilling tears things up, kills off a lot of microorganisms, can pack the soil, and leads to wonderful crops of weeds.

So... it's really bad, right?
Not so fast!

Why Tilling Is Good

Now here's the part that will make that hippie down the street mad at me. I'm going to tell you why tilling can also be a good practice.

Imagine you need to feed a lot of people quickly. Are you going to be able to gather enough mulch or plant a cover crop and scythe it down in time?

No. You need to plant right now. So you borrow a tractor or get a tiller and go to town. In one afternoon you can prepare a large planting space. This is where tilling really shines: it's fast.

When it comes to feeding people, I'm totally okay with throwing microorganisms under the bus. Tilling and planting a quarter-acre in a day is quite possible. Try doing that with mulch! Forget it. The outside input required becomes ridiculous if you go large-scale with most no-till gardening methods. If your garden is like that of Paul Gautschi, the *Back to Eden* guy, and you make friends with a tree company, great. But for most of us... that's a hard row to not hoe.

No-till advocates will point to the Dust Bowl and talk about how much soil and organic matter is lost when you till—and they're correct to an extent. If you keep turning the ground over and over again, you will see a loss of humus and a decrease in soil structure. Tilling at the wrong time can also wreck a plot. That's why tilling needs to be linked with "green manuring" the ground. If you grow buckwheat, legumes, cereal rye, and other cover crops and till them under to add organic matter back to the ground, you'll be able to repair the damage you've done and increase soil fertility at the same time.

There's a right and wrong way to till, but there's no reason why tilling can't be added to your gardening toolkit. I can respect being a purist, but there is a time for everything... even "evil" things, like tilling. If I can borrow a tractor or rent a tiller and get a big beautiful garden created in a weekend, I will do it. Especially when we're talking survival gardening.

Later in this book we'll take a look at grid-down tilling, but for now, let's look at another ground-breaking method.

Double-Digging

It seems almost everyone (except for those stubborn, old-fashioned farmers) has ditched row gardening and big spaces for tight little controlled boxes of heavily irrigated plants in perfect soil. Considering how many people live in tight little controlled boxes, perhaps this makes some sense.

If you like high yields from small spaces and are willing to spend the extra time watering, standard raised beds are not the only option. There's a much cheaper method that, though laborious, works wonders in every soil in which I've tried it.

Without buying lumber, nails, or soil, you can create an excellent 5 x 8-foot bed in about an hour.

What is this magical Third Way? Double-dug Biointensive™ gardening. Get ready to bust some sod.

The complete biointensive approach is useful for getting a productive garden going on the cheap. In fact, it's been used in Kenya and elsewhere for that very reason. Based on the pioneering work of English master gardener Alan Chadwick and improved upon by John Jeavons, this method relies on double-digging, compost, and close planting of veggies to keep the soil loose, fertile, and moist. John Jeavons's book *Grow More Vegetables* is a wealth of information on this method. Some biointensive gardening ideas you'll run across are out of left field and include planting by the lunar cycle and burying quartz-filled cow horns in your garden. This comes from the method's link to biodynamic farming, which has aspects of mysticism and New Age spirituality mixed in with plant growing. However, you don't have to buy in to the entire biointensive thing in order to learn from the basic method. Some of its tenets, like super-close crop planting, frequent watering, and novel approaches to spacing and fertilization are not part of my routine. I've also never been able to get close to the yields projected in Jeavons' book. However, there is one aspect that really impressed me when I tested it out. That aspect is double-digging. Double-digging is powerful.

Why Double-Digging Works

When we look at our plants, we tend to think only about what we see. If the growth above ground is green and happy, great! Unfortunately, that's only half—or less than half—of the picture. Root growth is very important to the health of a plant and its ability to stand drought stress, find nutrients, and keep itself supported. When you use a tiller you are really only ripping up the top 6 inches or so of the ground. Beneath that, the soil might still be hard and unyielding to roots. Mulching deeply can loosen soil over time by attracting worms that aerate for you. But if you really want to get your gardens going in a hurry, double-digging is the way to put food on the table ASAP.

Do you realize that some vegetable roots will penetrate as deeply into the ground as you are tall? You'd never know it if you yank up a little plant, but the complete collection of its roots are much more impressive than what you see. Loosen the soil deeply, and much more water and nutrients become available to the ever-searching (and sometimes microscopic) roots of your crops. Plus, having air in the soil is a good thing. Roots need to breathe.

With moderate watering and weeding, double-dug gardens do very well. I was quite pleased with the results in mine, especially since I wasn't sure how the method would work in my sandy yard. Six months after I dug my initial double-dug beds and three months after I harvested them, the soil, though weedy, was still fluffy and loose. A year later they were still softer than the surrounding ground. It only took a little weeding and raking, and they were ready to plant again.

When I moved to the Caribbean and tried the same method in hard clay, it worked just as well there too. Don't walk on your beds, and they'll serve you well for quite a while before needing a re-dig.

Now let's take a look at how you double-dig.

How to Double-Dig

Haven't double-dug before? You are in for a good workout. To do it, first pick out a space to attack. I like 4-foot wide beds for ease of reach from either side, though John Jeavons recommends going to 5 feet for the sake of creating a garden "microclimate" when the leaves touch. Once you determine the width, you can make a bed as long as you like.

Once you have your bed dimensions marked (I put bricks at the corners for visual reference), start removing the weeds, rocks, old boots, soda cans, and other debris. A grape hoe is a good tool for this (more on grape hoes later), but you can use a shovel as well. If you plan way ahead, you can also cover a patch of ground with a tarp during the warm season and let that kill off all the weeds for a few months.

Once your space is relatively cleared of weeds, it's time to start digging. Begin by making a foot-deep trench across the width of the bed at one end and put the removed dirt into a wheelbarrow or some buckets.

Now take a spading fork and use it to loosen the soil in the bottom of the trench you've just dug. Push it into the ground to the entire length of the tines, then rock back and forth to break up the ground. This is easy in sand but tough in clay.

Your first trench completed, do the same thing in the next strip, taking that soil and shoveling it into the adjoining furrow. Continue digging, loosening, and filling until you reach the last trench. When that one is also loosened to a depth of roughly 24 inches, dump in the soil you dug out of the very first trench. Now you have a beautiful, loose patch of soil, all ready for seeds or transplants. If you wish to add compost, you can do so while digging or simply sprinkle it onto the surface of the bed and rake it in. I often add cottonseed meal, compost blood meal, manure, bone meal, crushed eggshells, and other amendments to the top of the bed and rake it around, then plant the bed and water it all in.

With proper double-digging, your new garden will usually end up 4 to 6 inches taller than the adjoining unloosened soil. The fluffiness and tilth beat the living daylights out of anything you can do with a rototiller.

And again, after you've done all this work, don't step on it! Avoiding soil compaction is key to higher yields. When roots grow easily, plants thrive.

The work involved with double-digging is not inconsiderable, but it's good work. It's healthy exercise that leads to a great outcome. Your plants will appreciate your labor and reward you with abundant yields.

So, What Works for You?

Which gardening style you choose will depend on your climate, your health, the size of your land, and your access to water.

If you have a lot of space, tilling up a big patch and planting row crops makes a lot of sense. If you have limited access to water, this also makes sense since wide rows with wider spacing are more tolerant of low water than raised or double-dug beds. If you plant your corn 6 inches apart in 12-inch wide rows, they will wilt if they go without water for several days because all the roots in the bed are competing for a limited resource. If they're spaced wider, the roots have more area in which to hunt for moisture.

I've grown corn without irrigation in a sandy field at 3-foot spacing between rows of corn planted 12 inches apart. I was amazed by how well it did. That same corn would have done terribly in a square foot garden without supplemental water. Later, I tested single-row gardening with daikons, mustard, cabbages and other crops and it did very well. Even when you just till 6" deep and plant in single rows with some 10-10-10 and 3' spacing between, you'll do well. Wive spacing makes for less resources required and less water inputs.

The other benefit of growing like a farmer with long rows is that you can grow a lot of food without having to put in borders or spend a lot of time digging. Hoeing the rows is easy in a big garden if you have a wheel hoe (more on those soon). On the downside, some needier plants definitely do better in a highly improved intensive garden. For straight up production when you have more land, garden like a small farmer with nice long rows.

If you have a smaller space, raised beds and biointensive plots make more sense. They allow you to cram a lot more plants into less ground. Add creative trellises to let some of your gardening go vertical, and you'll really be rocking the yields. The close spacing of your crops actually helps keep the weeds down by shading the soil and choking out the competition. The downside is the need for more water along with the labor involved in preparing the soil. Even with those considerations, biointensive beds in particular are much easier to feed organically than larger row gardens. It takes a lot less compost for the same results. If you were to try and feed a giant row garden with manure, you'd be doing a *lot* of shoveling for a *long* period of time. Smaller, tighter, plant-packed beds take some of that time-consuming materials handling out of the picture.

In my gardens I mix multiple methods. When we lived with less space, we stuck to double-dug or at least broad-forked (We'll get to broadforks soon!) beds. When I have more space, I also add wide rows.

The key to gardening success is practice, patience, and experimentation. Get started now! Try a few different methods, and you will find success.

Chapter 2

How Much Space Does It Take?

"Can you feed yourself off your land?" That question comes up over and over again on homesteading forums, in farming discussions, and amongst preppers. The answers usually range from "heck no" to "sure, I could like, do it tomorrow, man."

Throw both of those answers out. The first guy is a defeatist—and the second guy is almost certainly exaggerating.

Once you accept that it is indeed possible to feed yourself off a piece of land, the second question is: how much land? That's where things get really tricky. You have to ask yourself a few questions first. Let's handle those one at a time before digging deeper.

Personal Question #1:
How much time do you have?

Are you thinking you're gonna grow all your calories between your job delivering pizza and your many other responsibilities? If you're tight on time, you might want to just work more hours and snag the rejected pineapple/salami/onion/anchovy experiments the cook likes to make between orders. It takes some serious hours to plan, plant, slaughter, harvest, feed, water, etc. If civilization collapses, you may have more time. And less pizza.

Personal Question #2:
Are you willing to work like a madman?

Growing your calories isn't easy. They don't fall into your hands. We're not living in the Garden of Eden anymore. We have to work like crazy, no matter what people tell you about amazing irrigation systems, earth boxes, or their friend that grows buckets of tomatoes in just minutes a day. Finding ways to save some work are really important, but you are still going to have to work. Can your back handle it? Will you do it?

Personal Question #3:
Will you actually eat what you grow?

I'm amused by people who grow gardens and yet live on soda, chips, etc. Their food growing is a hobby; it's not a major part of their diet. You'll recognize these folks because they're the ones giving away lots of produce rather than canning it. They're the ones who complain about the "mess" created by their apple tree out front. They're the ones who love to grow a few jalapeños and a tomato plant on the patio. It's a good start... but unless you're willing to eat in season, dehydrate food, plus can and make your produce a big part of your day-to-day calories, forget it. Drop the soda and drink your own cider from that "messy" tree, and you'll be on the right path. Eventually you'll have to do it anyhow. Why not start now?

Assuming that you have time, a desire to work, and the desire to actually eat what you grow, now you need to figure out what it will take to grow it. The first question—as I mentioned above—is almost always "how much space does it take?"

That's a huge question and requires you to ask yourself a few more questions.

Land Question #1:
What does your rainfall/water supply look like?

If you're growing in an arid region, you're going to need a lot more space. Some years ago I grew two patches of corn without irrigation. One patch was spaced at 18 inches between rows, the other was spaced at 36 inches between rows. The first patch did well; the second was stunted and failed to produce many good ears. Many people have this idea that gardening in wide rows is something home gardeners adopted from factory farming. The thought is: "Hey, that's the extra space machinery needs for access and harvesting."

However, that's not actually true. Yes, tractors need some space, and before that, mules and plows needed space, but I think the main reason old-school gardens had that huge spacing was because the plants needed all the water they could

get.　Generous root spacing lowered competition between
plants and ensured they'd survive in a time without easy access
to water.　Imagine watering a cornfield with buckets from a
creek, and it makes sense.　My experiment was a test of the
ground's water-holding capacity.　Your land will vary.　If you
live in the rainforest, you can plant really tightly.　If you're in
Arizona, you're going to need a lot more space between plants.

Land Question #2:
What is your climate?

In much of the tropics, feeding yourself is really easy.　There
are no seasons to speak of, other than dry and rainy times.
You've got a massive diversity of food crops to pull from—
and many of them produce year-round or at least repeatedly
through the year.　Ever wonder why bananas are always available at about the same price in the store?　They're basically
non-seasonal.　Sweet potatoes are also a perennial in the
tropics: plant them here and there when you please, then dig
now and again when you feel like it.　Fruits, nuts, and pretty
much everything grows really fast down there.　When plants
don't have to deal with freezes and fighting to get all their
reproduction done in a few warm months of growing time,
they can get plenty of food-making done.

On the other extreme, if you're in some place like Alaska,
you're going to have to deal with a short season of getting
things done in the garden and packing away as much as

possible while the sun shines. There's a reason the Inuit lived on seals, fish, whale, and other game rather than on veggies.

Land Question #3:
What is the fertility of your soil?

If you've got rich, deep, loamy topsoil, growing is easy. If you're hacking into yellow nutrient-depleted clay, growing is tough. It takes a lot more land if the land is poor. In the case of really bad land, you might want to concentrate on livestock—like goats, which can take weeds and brush and turn them into human food—rather than on growing lots of crops. Think nomadic herdsman, not farmer. You'll be healthier than a heavy carb-eater, too.

But How Much Space Does It Take?

If you've answered the questions above, you've made a good start toward figuring out the space. Theoretically, no matter what the climate, if you were willing to make radical changes in your diet, you could probably live on an average suburban lot. How so?

MEALWORMS AND SPIRULINA!!!

Yes, that would feed you. However, most of us don't want to do that. We'd rather eat meat, eggs, veggies, and fruit.

Let's be serious: this takes space. With a big one-acre garden, two acres for goats, and another two acres for your orchards, food forest, chickens, ducks, ponds, etc., you could live pretty well in a good climate on good dirt. In the tropics, you can live well on an acre or less. In rough dry land, you might be talking 20 or even 100 acres. It's all a matter of how creative you are and what you grow/raise. I'm constantly amazed by the diversity some permaculture gardeners (if you're not familiar with permaculture, go look it up!) are able to pack into tiny spaces.

Sometimes being limited is a good thing! We tend to think "Dang... I need a lot of space..." then we get a bunch of space and fail to utilize it well. I encourage people who are just starting out to pick a little space, make it as amazing and productive as possible, then expand. Scatter-shot approaches can work on big areas, but you may be surprised by how much you can do in just a little space. (For inspiration, check out the Dervaes family and their Urban Homestead.)

Every geographical area (except perhaps the Sahara) is able to support something edible. If your neighbors are doing great growing peanuts but poorly at cabbage, you might want to concentrate on legumes.

Now let's take a look at a few homestead staples you should try. All of the crops I'm going to discuss have different yields and space requirements, but through constant experimentation, you will figure out what works best.

Grains are the first thing most of us think about when we think about feeding ourselves. Yet that's one of the last places we should turn (with the notable exception of corn, which I'll cover later), for calories in small-scale homesteading. The labor and space required is somewhat ridiculous. Yeah, it can be done—and I've done it on a small scale—but by the time you get enough seeds together, the loaf of bread you'll make was totally and utterly not worth the effort. Are you ready to hook up a plow, sow, buy a scythe, cut, bundle wheat into sheaves, pray it doesn't rain, rub the husks off, chuck grain into the air on a breezy day to get rid of the chaff, and then grind the stuff? This is why the Irish loved the potato. Roots are your friends.

Where I live, I grow malanga, cassava, Seminole pumpkins, calabazas, potatoes, boniato, icicle radishes, daikons, garlic, true yams, sweet potatoes, turnips, beets and carrots. Up north I grew a huge bed of Jerusalem artichokes, beets, potatoes, Hubbard squash, leeks, grain corn, green onions, radishes, onions, and horseradish. Many roots will stay in the ground beyond the short harvests of other crops. Try leaving tomatoes on the vine - no dice. Forget to pick green beans? The plant gives up.

Roots are much more forgiving and should play a key role in keeping you fed. After roots, squashes, greens, and beans will keep you going.

The Three Sisters

We may think of pumpkins and squash as nice decorations in fall, but for American Indians and the pioneers who followed them, squash meant survival. Many of the old winter squash varieties are large and can store for six months or longer. If you've got the climate and the space for these powerhouses, growing storable squash should be a priority. Likewise, dry beans are a good source of storable protein. Nab old-school shell beans, and try a variety on your land. Though their yield isn't as good as some survival plants, beans will repair your land by adding nitrogen. Crop them between other species, and count the beans as an extra bonus.

A particularly good plant to mix with beans and squash is the old standby: corn. Sweet corn isn't what you want for survival. You want old grain varieties such as Hickory King, Bloody Butcher, or Hopi Blue. Think scrappy, tough and uncorrupted by genetic modification. Grits, corn meal, corn bread, and polenta corn—these are staple foods. Unlike other grains, corn is easy to harvest. Intercrop it with squash and beans in the "Three Sisters" method, and you'll get much more use of your space—plus confuse pests.

Do you have wild areas beyond the edges of your cultivated space? Identify useful species and encourage them. I found wild plums, black cherries, wild grapes, and other edibles after moving to my property. Though these are low-yield plants, they're also sources of food I don't have to work for. Add to them the wide variety of uncultivated edible greens that pop up during various seasons, and you've got something to nibble most of the year. From blackberries to puffball mushrooms and boletes, smilax shoots (also known as greenbrier), to black walnuts, figure out what's out there and how to use it. Think like Sacagawea.

Chickens

Say you're sick of potatoes. That's when you're going to want an animal to turn those tiresome veggies into something sustaining. Enter the chicken. Eggs are simply one of the best things you can eat, despite the cholesterol Nazis. They're rich in vitamins and minerals, plus protein and fat, and will fill you up better than vegetables alone. The problem with raising chickens is that you need to feed them as well as yourself. Unless you have a good stretch of free-range pasture/woods and a nice patch of food just for them, you're going to have to buy feed... and yet again, you're not self-sufficient. There has to be a balance between bird population and feed. For a family of four, I'd shoot for 6–8 laying hens and one rooster to protect them and provide you with the next generation of birds. Chickens don't need much space, so I'd add them directly after my gardens get established. I'd also go for tough homestead dual-purpose breeds that are good at foraging, not for something cutesy like cochins, bantams, or other silly show birds.

But How Much Space Does It Take, Dang It?

Basically, if you concentrate on calorie crops and grow as much as you can in tight beds, I'd wager a 4,000 square foot garden could keep you going on 2,600 calories a day.

That said, only you can figure out the exact space you need on your land in your climate, and with your own abilities and time. Start with heavily utilizing what you have and concentrating on high-yield crops such as roots. Then move on to squash, beans, and corn. Then add chickens and learn to forage for wild edibles. Beyond that, don't forget good producers such as cabbage, kale, and green beans. (And, don't worry—we'll talk more on specific crops in an upcoming chapter, so sit tight.)

If you have a little more space, pack in a food forest or an orchard and get long-term tree crops rolling, including health-packed berries and nuts. I did a lot of this on one acre, then later on a half-acre. Through the beginning of the pandemic, we went for many months without going to the grocery. Though we're not self-sufficient yet, we know we can go for some months without buying any food if need be. And as the trees mature and the perennial root crops really get going, that length of time will increase.

Though I'm a big fan of reaching the destination of completely feeding my family, the journey itself has been highly enlightening thus far. Every day we inch closer to the goal, and if you work hard, you will too. Do it now before you're forced to.

Chapter 3

Tools

"Shoot weeds up so high in the air that gravity incinerates them on the way back down!"

"Pick tomatoes with a handy extendable glove that also turns hornworms into SOLID GOLD, then sell them for CASH MONEY!"

"Gather biomass sustainably with this amazing tri-swiveling rake, now with Super Grass-Sculpting Action!"

Ever since the Garden of Eden, snakes have been trying to sell us things we really don't need.

I like tools, and I've worked in advertising, so I know why these promises are so enticing. Once you've double-dug a couple of garden beds, the thought of Effortlessly Aerating Your Lawn or Garden to a Depth of *6 Feet* with this So-Easy-a-Child-Could-Do-It EarthTwisterSuperWand™ has a certain appeal. In the past I've fallen for a couple of less-than-useful tools that promised bliss but brought only monetary regret.

Back when I lived in Tennessee I had thick, rocky clay in my backyard. The ground was so hard that it took me 15–

20 minutes to dig a hole big enough to plant a peach tree. Turning the soil was viciously hard to do, and breaking new seedbeds was a Sisyphean task.

One fine spring day I rented a big tiller and attacked a patch of lawn. Despite the tough soil and rocks, after three passes I had a reasonably decent place to plant that year's garden. It took $40, some gasoline, and a lot of arm-vibrating, skull-jarring, leg-tiring work. Not fun.

I wondered if there was a non-powered way to do this job.

Some time later that same year I came across a strange tool at Lowes. It was a twist cultivator of some sort. There was a pair of handles somewhat like those of a bike, connected to a shaft pointing downwards to a multi-tined head at the bottom. There was even a picture on the label of a happy woman barely straining as she fluffed up dirt. I could do that! No gas, no renting, no exhaust, no jarred teeth... just me, twisting and fluffing dirt in the sunshine like the pretty lady on the label. Hey, I could handle that.

So I bought it.

An hour later at home I attacked a little piece of my front planter. It turns out that the tines needed to be rammed into the ground like a Spartan spear... and once they were in the ground twisting wasn't easy. In fact, the tool was better for working my abdominal muscles than it was for working the soil.

Garden gadget fail.

Another failure was less related to looking for an easy way out and more about not seeing a better option. I once needed a new pair of long-handled loppers to do some clean-up work on one of my pear trees. I went to the garden center and started hunting. Most of the tools there were either cheaply made or too huge for what I wanted. The only pair that looked to be about the right size had telescoping handles. Okay, whatever. I would have preferred something simpler but the loppers were the right size. so I bought them.

After the first few minutes of actual trimming use, I was ticked. The handles had a bad habit of extending and retracting with every slight twist. When you are trying to gnaw through branches overhead, this is maddening. I took them back and bought a bow saw.

I've also had fights with string trimmers, bulb planters, electric chainsaws, tillers, and various other yard and garden accessories. There's a reason a lot of these tools are recent inventions: they're a product of a lazy consumer society mixed with companies looking for a gimmicky fast sale.

Sure, there are some great modern inventions (like the tractor) and there have been good innovations on old ideas (like the broadfork), but most of the best tools are centuries old. Unlike anything electrified or created to run on gasoline, these tools will also keep working for you no matter what happens to the economy or the supply lines.

These are the tools that will save your skin. I don't need extra nylon string for my machete. I don't need 10W/30 for my spading fork.

You know what they say: if it looks too good to be true, you're going to end up paying child support from behind bars.

No, that's not right... how did it go?

Ah yes: if it looks too good to be true, it probably is. Beware of tools that look complicated or promise amazing results. Even "simple" things like drip hoses can be a pain in the neck. If you want to garden well, get good tools, learn to use them well, and if you feel the urge to get something gadgety, make sure you can afford to burn that money.

Now let's take a look at the tools you really *should* have!

Tools for the Apocalypse

Ever consider what life might look like if fuel became rare, super-expensive, or both? Ever think about what the grocery store shelves would look like if shipping was disrupted? (We saw some of this back in 2020 - I'm looking at you, toilet paper hoarder!) Ever wonder what would happen if an EMP took out the grid? I have (usually while clutching a tumbler of Jim Beam and hiding under a mattress along with my 3,000 cans of baked beans).

With a single jolt to our supply lines, a lot of the things we rely on for daily life would no longer be reliable, and food would be at a premium. Gardening, at first glance, seems like it wouldn't be that hard without technology and fuel. But when you consider that most gardeners are relying on mowers, tillers, tractors, RoundUp™ and chemical fertilizers, we've got a problem.

Could you manage even a quarter-acre garden without gas? You can if you have the right tools—and you'll become healthier at the same time. How so? Because it's darned hard work! If everything collapses, good tools are must-haves. Get them now, and learn to use them before it's too late.

When things get ugly, you're going to want most of the following tried-and-tested tools for your garden. If you gather them together now and learn how they work, you won't be scrambling in the future.

Shovels and Spades

This one is a no-brainer; that's why it's at the top of the list. If you don't have a shovel, what's wrong with you? From burying carcasses and trenching in compost, to double-digging and dispatching zombies, you *need* a shovel. Get one. And get a good one. If you've got a bigger budget, get three. Grab a short-handled spade with a square blade for double-digging, a long-handled digging shovel, and a large square point shovel for mucking out chicken coops, scraping mulch off driveways, tossing around manure, etc.

The Spading Fork

When you mention the spading fork, people often wonder what in the world you're talking about. They're likely picturing a pitchfork or "manure fork" rather than this tough garden implement. The spading fork is a simple tool for double digging a new garden bed. By stomping its hard tines into the ground and working it back and forth, you aerate and break up compacted soil, giving plants a major advantage over those growing in unloosened soil. A spade and a spading fork together can prepare ground twice as well as a rotary tiller. It takes a lot longer, but the plants grow a lot better. Trust me— I've tried it both ways. There's no beating the deep reach of a spading fork.

Weeding Hoes

The standard hoe is the long-handled thing with a curved metal blade on a gooseneck that your dad kept in his shed for some unknown reason, rusting, unused, and unappreciated as a garden tool. Plenty of us have this idea that a hoe is a total pain in the neck to use. That's partly truth... and partly fiction. Yes, hoeing is tiring work, but that's often because we don't sharpen the blade and bend the gooseneck so the blade chops through weeds at a comfortable angle. Use a hoe to clean up the weeds around fruit trees, to hill up potatoes, and to weed between garden rows. A standard hoe is a useful implement, particularly in rocky, weedy. or clay-rich areas. But if you're got somewhat loose soil and weeding that needs doing, you'll also want to get the standard hoe's ugly sister, the "scuffle hoe."

Also known as the "hula hoe," this tool is a weed-eating machine. It has an oscillating blade that rocks back and forth, gliding through the soil and severing weeds just below the surface. If you maintain your gardens and don't allow the weeds to get too big and thick, regular clean-ups with a scuffle hoe are a piece of cake. My wife and I both use this tool all the time. It's easy to control and doesn't require the tiresome chopping motion of a standard hoe.

Another hoe worth mentioning is the "grape hoe." Unlike the standard hoe, the grape hoe has a wide, heavier blade that covers a lot of ground quickly. You can even use it to clear sod, thanks to its strong steel blade. When you chop with this, things happen quickly. Originally used in vineyards, this is an excellent tool for homesteaders growing any variety of crops.

The Grub Hoe

The grub hoe predates tillers, gasoline, and the Industrial Revolution. It's simple, tough, and indispensable for gardening and tilling by hand. Grub hoes are common in much of the world but rather scarce in the United States for some reason. In the undeveloped world they're everywhere.

Unlike a shovel, a grub hoe allows you to dig and turn earth with a minimum of effort. The longer, heavy blade's weight throws dirt at a rapid pace. I've used grub hoes to till new ground, to plant trees, and even to dig and shape a small pond.

The heavy head and the angle of a grub hoe works with you, ensuring that you don't have to put a lot of effort into your swing as you chop down into the earth. If you have to till a large area without access to gasoline or draft animals, a grub hoe is your tool. It wouldn't be nearly as easy as a tractor, but it'll be there when the tractor no longer runs.

I recommend the grub hoes sold at www.easydigging.com. The price is excellent, and the quality is high.

For tilling off-grid, the grub hoe works excellently, though its reach doesn't go as deep as that of a broadfork. It busts through tough weeds and sod that would choke a consumer-grade rototiller. I can get down to 12 inches without too much trouble in my sandy loam, but your local conditions will vary. I wish I had this tool back when I was dealing with thick Tennessee red clay! I'm sure it would've torn up my hands, but I also could have made a good dent in a lot less time than trying to dig with a shovel.

Using a grub hoe isn't hard, but it's still work, no matter what your soil type. You will get winded if you attack the ground with vigor; however, if you pace yourself, tilling by hand is a truly productive exercise, unlike riding a stationary bike.

The Ridging Hoe

The ridging hoe (also known as an azada or a triangular hoe) is a pointed hoe made for wreaking serious havoc and taking no prisoners.

The pointed blade cuts into the ground with very little effort due to its shape, allowing weeds to be removed rapidly. It's also the best hoe for creating planting furrows for seeds and potatoes. For quick hand tilling, this tool also excels. It's easier than the grub hoe though it doesn't move quite as much earth at a time. It's also not as good for chopping roots.

If you want a delicate weeding hoe, this isn't it. But if you need a way to tear through the ground fast (goodbye lawn?), this tool will get you started quickly. I also got mine from www.easydigging.com, since their tool quality is much higher than most retailers I've seen, and because they're one of the very few places that actually carries this handy hoe.

The Wheel Hoe

Some years back, I discovered an old school tool called a "wheel hoe." It's basically an oscillating hoe, also known as a scuffle hoe or hula hoe, with a wheel (or a pair of wheels) in front of it and two handles. With a wheel hoe you can slice through weeds much faster than you can with a hand-held hoe. You get extra leverage from the wheel and handles, too. With tall weeds, the hoe tends to choke up and needs regular clearing, but with short ones it's a champ. I once used a wheel hoe on a piece of lawn as a test. Yes, you can clear it one chunk at a time, but it will *kill* you. A wheel hoe is made for using in already worked soil. It's a clean-up tool that's not really suitable for breaking ground, but it will allow you to weed a huge area in a very short period of time. I use ours every week or two between my annual garden beds, and it's a very quick and satisfying tool.

My main go-to wheel hoe is the Planet Whizbang wheel hoe which you used to be able to buy as a kit from the amazing homesteading madman Herrick Kimball. Unfortunately, he's discontinued making them.

If you want to get fancy, the Hoss wheel hoe has all kinds of great blades, mounding attachments and even a well-designed seeder for large gardens. I got my Hoss wheel hoe from www.easydigging.com (yes, I really like that company!) and find it to be an amazing tool. Though it's not as simple and fast as my Planet Whizbang wheel hoe, it's a lot more versatile. Glaser also makes a nice-looking wheel hoe based on the old Planet Jr. models, though I have not tried one yet. They are sold by Johnny's Selected Seeds.

Bow Rake

Also known as a "hard-tined" rake, this tool is perfect for leveling newly dug beds. It's a weed-sifting machine, a young weed eliminator, a seed-burier and, in the proper hands, a formidable Ninja weapon. Like the shovel, this is a no-brainer tool. Get one.

Leaf Rake

I use a metal-tined leaf rake for most of my gardening work. When I've turned an area over, this is the tool I use for the final polish on a bed. It has a much lighter touch than the bow rake and isn't any good at pulling dirt around. One great use for a leaf rake is—you guessed it—raking leaves. If things get ugly, you'll need to rake up big piles of leaves and grass clippings for your compost pile, and this is the go-to tool. The big plastic rakes work as well, but do not last as long.

Hand sickle

This is very useful for cutting tall weeds, grain stalks, and greenery. I use mine regularly. It's also an antique.

Machete

This is my favorite tool ever. It's perfect for clearing vines and brush. It also makes you look cool.

The key to machete success is keeping that sucker sharp. I run a file down mine almost every time I use it. A good edge makes the blade sing. Machetes are great for cleaning up bamboo or branches for tomato stakes, decapitating chickens for the table, and clearing cornstalks. I've also used one to chop-and-drop mulch plants in my food forest, as well as for punching holes in the garden for transplanting seedlings. (Granted, a trowel may have worked better, but I would've had to walk all the way to my barn for that.)

My favorite style of machete is the classic "cane machete." My model has a good heft and a hook that's useful for pulling branches and vines, plus the top is squared off rather than pointed, which gives each swing more power. I also cut through two tendons with it once, so be careful. Wearing a broad-brimmed straw hat while using a machete with a hook on the back which is perfect for catching the edge of a broad-brimmed straw hat thereby redirecting a swing downwards into the back of one's hand does not make for safe chopping.

Pruning Shears/Loppers

These are great for pruning fruit trees and dealing with downed limbs. Short-handled pruning shears are for precision work like taking cuttings and pruning small branches; the long-handled loppers allow you a lot more leverage to remove branches up to 1.5 inches thick.

Broadfork

The broadfork is a startlingly efficient tool for loosening the soil to depths in excess of 12 inches, depending on the design. Though most broadforks (with the notable exception of the Meadow Creature broadfork) aren't made for breaking new ground, they can do it in a pinch if you don't have conditions that are too rough. Hard clay, rocks, and roots may bend or break weaker broadforks.

Though double-digging is probably a better way to create new garden beds, you can cover a *lot* more ground with a lot less work by using a broadfork.

Don't get me wrong: I love firing up a tiller and destroying vast swaths of grass and weeds. It looks like you've made a ton of progress when you till, yet the ground has really only been loosened to a depth of about 6 inches. Additionally, you are tearing through countless earthworms, good insects, and beneficial fungal nets as you go. Wait a week or two, and the weeds will pop right back up. You'll be out there tilling again, murdering whatever earthworm refugees managed to survive your first pass—and who knows what you're doing to the soil on a microscopic level! Mass genocide! The Agents of FADAM are gonna get you!

Using a broadfork helps you avoid all the carnage and get deeper into the ground at the same time. It's hard work; there's no way around that. It's worthwhile, however, and isn't really as difficult as you might think. Besides, being a fat pansy is no way to go through life. Broadforking is good for you, much like cod liver oil, fresh air, and a good clean fistfight.

The first time out is the toughest. You'll find yourself getting into the feel of the tool and rolling along until the next thing you know, you have blisters and a sore back. A few days later, you'll be tough enough to do a lot more. Then eventually it's no big deal at all. My wife, who is a thin slip of a gal, can broadfork for an hour without quitting.

The way a broadfork works is simple. It's a two-handled fork with multiple tines pointing downward. The operator picks the tool up by the handles and drops or thrusts the tines into the soil as deep as they'll go without pushing. He then stands on the bar at the top of the tines and starts rocking back and forth while gripping the handles. The tines usually have a slight curve that helps them work into the ground. After a few good rocks back and forth, the tines are buried completely in the ground. At that point, the user pulls back on the handles, drawing them down to ground level. The leverage breaks and loosens the soil with little effort. He then takes a step back and drops the tool into the ground again a few inches behind the previous impact point.

Yanking up fistfuls of normally stubborn weeds is easy after the broadfork has done its work beneath the surface. The deep loosening of the soil helps your plants grow good, strong root systems.

If you do buy a broadfork, don't skimp and get a cheap one. It will break and make you mad. A good fork is going to cost you around $200 unless you can weld, in which case it's very possible to make your own. I own the Meadow Creature broadfork because it was the toughest one I could find; however, I haven't tried every brand.

If I lost my broadfork somehow, or heaven forbid it was stolen by some sort of organic farming bandit, I'd buy another in a heartbeat.

Wheelbarrow

When you need to get stuff from one place to another, this is the way. I use both a classic one-wheeled wheelbarrow (which excels in gracefully transporting compost into the garden and through tight spaces) and a four-wheeled garden cart. I wouldn't want to lose either of them. Get a good quality wheelbarrow, and it will last a long time. I found mine in the dumpster of a K-Mart some years ago. The tire was flat, hence its untimely demise. I fixed it, and got an almost-free and much needed tool for the garden. When I double-dig my garden beds, I use the wheelbarrow as a repository for the dirt I take from the first row, then cart it around to the other end of the bed when I'm done with the last row. It works for hauling chicken feed, carrying leaves to the compost pile, holding piles of weeds as you work your beds, and carting laughing children around the yard.

Scythe

If you know how to use this graceful tool, it's almost as good as a lawnmower. A "bush" or "brush" blade will allow you to clear rough ground and vegetation, whereas a "grass" blade is much finer and will ding easily if it encounters stiffer opposition. Along with a scythe, you also need to own a good whetstone, plus a peening hammer and some sort of anvil to keep that super-fine scythe blade in shape.

I confess: I'm not great with a scythe, but I do own and know how to use one and keep the blade going in a pinch. There are experts on scythes that will blow your mind; I'm just not one of them. I bought an antique American-style scythe with an Austrian blade that can clear a path in a pinch, especially when I don't feel like running out to buy more string or gas for my string trimmer. If I have gas and a string trimmer, though, it's easier to just run with that. Grid-down, though, I'm going grim reaper.

What to look for when buying tools

Buy good stuff. Cheaper is not better. If it feels flimsy, is gadgety or trendy, or is made of plastic, avoid it. Antique shops are excellent sources for tough vintage tools. Forged heads on spading forks and shovels are really hard to find, but they're worth getting if you can. My best standard hoe is an antique one with a forged head. It takes a serious edge, has a perfect heft, and, despite its worn state, does a killer job.

Garage sales are another good place for finding garden tools. If it's in working shape and at a decent price, buy it—even if you already have one. Backups are a good idea.

Finally, remember: the supply of tools will also dry up during TEOTWAWKI. Don't get caught short.

Chapter 4

Irrigation

Water is the key to life. I know it's true, because that's what I read in the literature I got from this chick who was hawking some kind of ionized water.

Anyhow, if water isn't the key, it's at least the ignition, gas tank, chassis, windows, pistons, and alternator of life. Life doesn't work very well without water—plant life included—so one of your primary concerns on a survival-oriented homestead needs to be hoarding as much water as possible.

If things get ugly, you're going to need water for yourself, for your animals, and your garden.

Rain Barrels

Rain barrels are the hip thing to do these days. It's green! It's sustainable! Blah blah blah. It's gotten so silly that you can buy designer models at places like Target and totally blow your whole month's beans and rice budget on a single purchase. Of course, that purchase will look like it's made from RealFauxStone™ with hand-engraved niblets. If that's important to you, go for it. You can hide your Baby Glock beneath it and set the thing up while listening to Billy Joel's greatest hits.

It is good to have a rain barrel because they are an extra water source in case of grid collapse, plus they can save you a few cents on your water bill. It doesn't need to be anything amazing. My rain barrels cost me $16.00 each. I bought some used barrels that had formerly contained a (hopefully) non-toxic water treatment polymer that looked like horrible semi-translucent mucus but stickier, then I bought a little silicone and some brass spigots and cut the tops to allow the rain from my gutters to get in them. Over the hole in the top, I glued some metal window screening to keep the mosquitoes out. Simple. Just make sure you get spigots that have a wide open flow. I've bought some that don't let enough water through, and they will gum up easily with algae and debris. Plus they take way too long to fill a watering can.

Once you have your rain barrels, raising them up is a good idea. If you do, gravity will provide the water pressure you need to reach plants farther away. I once had a two-story house. I put my rain barrel on an 8-foot platform at one corner of the roof, and the pressure was excellent.

That said—not all is roses and candy. The main problem with rain barrels is that they don't hold enough water. One little shower, and they're overflowing. A roof can seriously catch a lot of water... and if you want to hold on to that water, you need to step up.

If you have a 1500-gallon tank, you'd be able to water your gardens for a long time. One nice rainfall, and that sucker would be full. Roofs are water-catching machines. Put the container at the top of a slope or on a platform and the extra pull of gravity will even let you water with a hose.

In the Caribbean almost every house had a cistern, and they were a lot bigger than the little rain barrels we have here. There, people know that the government may not be able to keep their water on in an emergency. When we moved there, we did the same thing, adding big tanks to our house. How high is your trust level?

Ponds and Pools

Pond-building is an art all its own. I've fiddled around with it, but my sandy soil here makes building a conventional clay-lined pond an expensive pain. I also don't like the cost of proper pond liners, plus I have little children, and I don't want them drowning one afternoon. So, instead of in-ground ponds, I've used the cast-away debris of our soulless consumer society to keep extra water around for the homestead. What kind of cast-off debris? Old jacuzzis! I have three of them right now, filled with fish and pond plants.

If you're really clever and like to burn lots of time and effort, you can turn your pond into a full-on aquaponics system, but I'm not really clever. I'm satisfied with a few edible plants, 10-cent feeder goldfish from the pet store, and a few mosquito fish from a local pond. They eat the mosquito larvae and manage to live in un-aerated water. If you're lucky enough to have a large in-ground pool, you can do the same with that in a pinch... unless you're planning on having bikini and beer parties throughout TEOTWAWKI. If so, please send an invitation to:

> David The Good
> c/o Econopocalypse Ranch
> 6078 Tick Road
> Sticksville, FL

Ready-made ponds can be made from basically anything that holds water. Except for that excuse you're gonna make to not invite me to your party.

To make these things work, I first unscrewed the various fixtures inside the hot tubs that could be unscrewed, then bought PVC screw-in caps that fit the hole sizes, adding teflon tape when I did so. Some of the holes in the hot tub were shaped strangely so I used pieces of cast-off acrylic plastic from an old racing go-cart windshield (some sort of plexiglass/lucite) that I cut with my bandsaw to cover the holes with some good overlap, then I used aquarium silicone to glue them into place. It took a little work and a couple of failed, leaking experiments, but it worked great in the end.

To get started with some soil for the bottom, I culled potted plants from my nursery that were doing poorly. I didn't want to use new soil or dig a bunch of sand up, so I just chucked the contents of dirt, weed, and dead plant-filled pots in there.

One of my hot tub ponds is near my barn. I was going to put a gutter off the barn roof to fill it... though I never actually got around to it. The rainfall has almost always been adequate to keep the hot tub ponds filled enough for my goldfish and various pond plants. On the few occasions where it's looked a bit low, I've topped it off with the hose, but no hot tub pond has really ever been in danger of drying out.

These ponds function as grid-down water storage, compost creation (via the vigorous pond plants I grow on the surface and regularly scrape off and chuck into the compost pile— more on that in my book *Compost Everything: The Good Guide to Extreme Composting*) and water gardening all in one. Check with your local hot tub/pool installer for cheap or free tubs. They often remove old hot tubs and trash them when they install new tubs. That means your hot tub pond will most likely end up being *free* if you catch the right person.

Or, just use your swimming pool like the Garden Pool folks did. Look them up at gardenpool.com.

Mulching and Double-digging

As I've written before, if you punch lots of good airspace into the ground via double-digging, the ground will hold more moisture when it rains... and when it doesn't.

Mulch is another way to keep things moist—particularly deep mulch. Pile it on, and pile it deep—just water really well first to make sure you're not blocking water from the ground with all that mulch.

Irrigation Without Electricity

I have a well that's powered by an electric pump. Even if you were on city water—what would happen if an EMP strike took out the grid? Would the water keep flowing? Would it be safe for watering your garden?

As I've written before, most modern gardening has been taken over by intensively planted raised beds. This method requires a lot of watering—and that watering will be really hard to do without running water—so think about water as you plan your gardening methods.

Just because the electric is gone, it doesn't mean you can't run your well. If you install a solar system now, you'll still be able to fill a pressure tank if the grid goes down... that is, unless an EMP blows out your solar system too. The next option for getting water out of your well is to install a manual pump. Unfortunately, that's not the easiest or cheapest thing in the world to do. Bison and Simple Pump both make deep-well hand pumps, but installation is a bit tricky, and the pumps are expensive. Of course, "expensive" is a relative term. How long could you live without water in your house? Spending a grand or two now would look brilliant if things ever went down.

I mentioned the hand-pump idea to one of my neighbors, who thought it was rather silly.

Neighbor: "Why not just run the pump with a generator?

Me: "Eventually, you run out of gas."

Neighbor: "We ran ours after the last hurricane without trouble. They got the power back on pretty quickly."

Me: "But what if they don't? What if the power is down for a long, long time?"

Neighbor: "Well..."

Me: "And what if I was kidnapped by the Brazilian women's beach volleyball team and couldn't buy gas because they made me their slave? I wouldn't be able to afford gas or even contact my family. All day and all night I'd be applying sunscreen... toweling... fetching cute little gym shorts... as a *slave*! Look—how would my family have anything to drink if they couldn't pump it out of the well? How can you *stand* living with yourself, neighbor? You really have no clue the *danger* I'm in! Any day now those awful predatory women could come and get me! Then what would you say, smarty pants? No water! No water!"

Neighbor: "I have to go now."

And there's the crux of the matter: installing a hand pump means you aren't stuck relying on gas to power your well. Even if you're forced against your will to travel to Rio at least your family will be able to get water for the garden. Hoping that someone fixes the grid in time—or that you can get enough gas—puts your water supply in the hands of others. If your water supply fails, your garden will too—as will your own body.

Now this is where you get to bare-bones simplicity. I live in a sandy patch of Florida where you'd think the ground would be terrible at supporting plants without irrigation; yet, right in my old North Florida neighborhood, there's a farmer named Jake who grows sweet potatoes, corn, watermelon, and other crops with only the rain that falls from the sky. The guy is tough as nails, wears a white hat, and looks like a cowboy. The first time I saw one of his fields of southern peas I thought, "Whoa, how is this guy managing this?" So I asked him.

His answer?

"I just grow with the rain the Good Lord sends me."

"But..."

Jake smiled. "My son is a preacher. I pay the Lord, and the Lord gives me rain. I always get just the rain I need."

"But..."

The secret to Jake's success, beyond "paying the Lord," starts to reveal itself when you take a good look at his fields. Rather than planting crops tightly, he has a generous 3-foot spacing between single rows. He also keeps the ground cultivated around his crops so the weeds can't suck away moisture.

Here's what we've managed to forget during our fat years of gardening with abundant irrigation and tight spacing: plants, especially certain plants, are capable of taking care of themselves better than you might think with much less water if they have enough room to do so. Root competition is fierce beneath the surface, and root systems can be remarkably extensive. Corn, for instance, can put roots 6–7 feet into the earth.

Wide spacing wasn't originally created for the sake of industrial machinery. It originated with observations made by farmers long before tractors arrived. When you have to carry water in buckets, making full use of rainfall becomes vitally important.

As I wrote before, wide spacing works! When plants are not fighting with their neighbors, their roots are pretty good at finding water and resources in the soil. You can help them out by loosening the ground with a broadfork or double-digging so your crops don't have to fight through hard subsoil to reach moisture. As we've already covered, double-dug beds conserve water significantly better than even perfectly amended non-dug raised beds. And, again, deep mulching is another option, if you have enough organic matter to pile on. I usually don't, so I save the mulch for perennials and trees.

Another way to maximize the water available to your plants: lightly hoe the surface of the ground after a hard rain. This breaks the capillary action and creates a "dust mulch" which will hold in water rather than letting it evaporate away. Note: you'll find a lot of information on dry farming in Steve Solomon's book *Gardening Without Irrigation*, which is available as a free e-book online.

If you have a slope, getting water to your crops is easy. If you don't, you're going to be stuck carrying water. If you have a flowing river or creek, you're really set—all you need is a water wheel or pump, and life is good provided you aren't going up a crazy slope.

In that case, you might want to invest in a burro and put a water tank on his back.

One method of irrigation for fruit trees and a limited amount of crops is to punch a small nail hole in the bottom of a five-gallon bucket, then place that bucket at the base of the plant you want watered. You'll have to carry water to it and pour it in, but the slow drip of the water from the bottom of the bucket is a great thing. Fill it with compost or manure tea (or pee in the bucket), and you'll add nutrients at the same time you water.

Irrigation via flooding is practiced in many countries, particularly on flat lands where it's possible to open a chute or re-direct a stream down ditches between your crops. It's an excellent method for watering but requires a pretty specific set of circumstances to work. If you had a large tank on the side of your house and soil that held water for a while, you could simply dig watering trenches between your crops and flood them via your saved rainwater. This would be difficult on a large scale but could work quite well in a small area.

If irrigation becomes a problem due to the grid shutting down, the easiest thing to do is just to do as Farmer Jake does: count on God to send rain from above. If you plan correctly and your climate allows, you may be able to grow quite a bit just on what falls from the sky in your field. It worked for thousands of years. Why not choose backup now, do some tests, and ask around before things get ugly? Some areas have spring rains and then no water through the year; others have dry springs and rainy summers. Some areas have rain year-round; others have very little. If you're dealing with a year-round low rainfall situation, you'll have to think through ways to carry water (a good yoke with two buckets is a good idea) but if you have the rainfall, learn to use it now before it's too late.

Chapter 5

Fertilizing

If water is the lifeblood of a garden, fertilizer is its bones.

Plants create quite a bit of what they need from sunlight; however, if the soil is lacking in nutrition, they'll fail to yield.

I've seen nicely tilled and weeded gardens with rows of well-watered but horribly stunted crops. There's one little garden in my neighborhood that I see all the time with half-sized plants. I can't tell you how often I've thought about throwing some manure or a water balloon filled with MiracleGro™ over the fence.

Imagine you lived on just water and oatmeal, how would you look? Probably about like those plants: sickly. In order to do well, you need a wide range of minerals. Calcium, iron, magnesium... a lot goes into a healthy body.

Plants are the same way, though their basic needs are a bit different than ours. For example, they don't need caffeine like we do.

The three "macro-nutrients" required by plants are nitrogen, phosphorus, and potassium, with nitrogen being the most utilized of the three. If you've ever bought a bag of fertilizer, you've seen the numbers on the bag: 10-10-10, 6-8-8, 27-0-0... these numbers are the "NPK analysis" of the fertilizer, giving the ratio of nitrogen, phosphorus, and potassium in that order: N=Nitrogen, P=Phosphorus, K=Potassium.

I remember, long, long ago, the first time I discovered the power of chemical fertilizer. I had been feeding plants here and there with compost, coffee grounds, etc., and they generally did well—yet it wasn't working on this sickly squash plant I'd planted in a pot on my front porch in the hopes it would climb up the wrought iron railings. I found an old bag of 10-10-10 in the carport of the house I was renting and put a tablespoon or so in the pot and watered it to see what would happen.

A few days later, it turned deep green and starting growing like Jack's beanstalk. Magic!

Chemical fertilizers definitely work wonders, but are they better than their organic counterparts?

Let's put them in the ring and make them fight!

Round 1:
In the Beginning Was Organic... and Then Came Science!

A long time ago, there were no "chemical" fertilizers as such. There was manure... animal carcasses... cover crops... ashes... nitrogen-fixing legumes... and that was about it. Before the tractor won the battle of Machine vs. Mule, most farms had lots of animals and lots of manure. This heady plant food was gathered and spread across fields, giving them plenty of long-term fuel for the growing season. Different crops were grown in different seasons and were turned into the soil after harvest. Sometimes various mined amendments were applied when farmers had access to them. Life was good, yields were decent, and the soil did well at supporting crops year after year. "Organic" amendments were the reigning champion because they had no competition.

In the 1800s, the brilliant chemist Justus von Leibig discovered that the main nutrient plants needed to grow was nitrogen. It was only a few short steps from there to realizing that a mix of nitrogen, phosphorus, and potassium (NPK) provided the main building blocks for plant growth—and only a few steps further to creating those nutrients synthetically. Chemical fertilization was born. It didn't take long to make inroads, especially since it meant you could grow crops in sub-par soil with much faster results and less work than using manure.

But that's enough background. Let's talk about the differences between chemical and organic and why they matter in your garden.

Round 2:
Organic Hits Back Hard!

When you go shopping for something to feed your plants, you quickly realize there are a lot of choices. Most of these revolve around various combinations of NPK: 6-6-6, 10-10-10 and 13-13-13 are considered "balanced" because they contain equal ratios of these macronutrients. The numbers are percentages, and the rest of the bag is usually comprised of filler material, unless it specifically states that it contains magnesium, copper, or other micronutrients. Scatter 10-10-10 around your garden, and the results are rapid and hard to argue with... until you start looking into the details.

Over time, the application of just chemical fertilizers has some negative results. Soil life is damaged by its salt content. Fillers may contain heavy metals and other toxins, and plants get used to the quick rush of fertilizer-induced growth and may not be as strong as their organic kin.

Sure, you can grow stuff in lousy soil with enough fertilizer, but the wide range of nutrients won't be present... meaning the produce you put on your table will be less healthy than produce grown in rich soil with organic amendments.

In recent years, occasional studies have appeared trying to convince us that factory-farmed, pesticide-laden, and chemically fertilized produce is just as good as its organic equivalent. The truth, however, is in the tasting. One bite out of a homegrown organic strawberry or a potato from the backyard will convince you there's more to healthy produce than corporate-funded studies that ignore the bland results of modern agriculture.

You can taste good food.

Though you don't have to go all hippie-freak in favor of organic amendments, there is one area in which many of them shine: they feed the soil as much as they feed the plant. What the heck does that mean? It means that the roots, worms, fungi, and millions of microorganisms that inhabit that dirt are more than the sum of their chemical parts. A healthy balance of lots of life in the ground leads to healthier plants, just as yogurt and other live-fermented foods help balance your digestive tract. Compost is particularly useful in this regard.

If you analyze compost like we analyze fertilizers, based on an NPK ratio, it looks pretty sad. Depending on original ingredients and where you look for data, the stuff usually doesn't crack 1-1-1. That's pathetic, right? Why would you want that crummy stuff on your gardens? The reason: living organisms are a lot more complicated than three simple numbers. Compost contains micronutrients from a wide variety of sources (which might include banana peels, watermelon rinds, leaves, grass clippings, eggshells, ramen noodles, hair, potato chips, coffee grounds, toenail clippings, etc.), rather than just a mix of the top three nutrients plants need for life. Compost also conditions your soil, unlike chemical fertilizers, by giving it humus. Humus is the persistent remains of organic matter that hold together and make the dirt fluffy and water-retentive. Though it doesn't act like plant caffeine—as 10-10-10 would do—it feeds slowly and well while inoculating your soil with a wide variety of microorganisms that work together in an amazingly designed way to keep plants healthy. Compost also attracts earthworms to the garden. Chemical fertilizers burn and chase them away. Getting the picture? There is more to plant life than NPK!

Beyond compost, there are other organic fertilizers that can kick your garden into high gear. Here are a few that work well:

Blood Meal

This is dried blood from slaughterhouses. Friday the 13th stuff. It's also nitrogen-rich and perfect for boosting needy plants like corn and leafy greens.

Bone Meal

Another meat industry by-product, bone meal is good for adding phosphorus. Phosphorus fosters healthy blooms and fruiting. It's also got calcium, which is another much-needed nutrient especially for tomatoes.

Fish Emulsion

Put sardines in the blender, then let them sit for a week and you'd get something that looks and smells like this stuff. It's got an amazing aroma, but it's also chock-full of nutrients that plants love. Are your plants lacking vigor? Mix some of this liquid into a watering can and dilute according to the manufacturer's directions, then water away. Pick up a copy of my book *Compost Everything: The Good Guide to Extreme Composting* if you want to start making your own fish emulsion at home. It's a *lot* cheaper than buying it!

Kelp Meal

Another product from the sea, kelp meal is packed with micronutrients, with some sources claiming it holds over sixty of the vitamins and micronutrients plants need. Throw this in your garden occasionally, or pick up seaweed at the shore, wash the salt off, and add it to your compost. You'll reap the mineral-rich bounty of the ocean.

Urine

Yep, you read that right. Did you realize urine has an NPK rating of roughly 15-1-2 which is comparable to commercial nitrogen fertilizers? Unfortunately, depending on your diet, it can also be high in salt. Dilute at about a 6 to 1 ratio of water to urine, then apply to plants. Urine, except in rare cases of infection, is sterile upon exiting your body, and it's *free*!

Cottonseed Meal

This is a byproduct of the cotton industry. It's another nitrogen-booster. I don't know if it's totally safe because of the genetically modified nature of most cotton as well as the pesticide and herbicide use, but it does work great in the garden and is technically organic. I've tilled it into a fall garden, then planted cabbages and had remarkable success.

Manure

Manures are one of the best things to feed your garden; however, with the exception of goat and rabbit manure, they need some time to age before you can put them in the garden. Chicken manure, in particular, is really hot stuff. Mix it directly into the compost pile or only use it for light side-dressing on nitrogen-sucking crops like corn. I'd keep it away from salad greens, though, to avoid bacterial contamination of your food. Beyond the realm of poultry, cow manure is really great stuff for the garden, as is rabbit manure. Horse manure is also decent but can be filled with weeds since horses don't have nearly the super-efficient digestive system of a cow.

Round 3:
Chemical Ain't Lookin' Bad...
and Organic Ain't Lookin' Perfect!

I mentioned manure above. However, many sources have now been contaminated with Aminopyralids and other long-term toxic herbicides. These poisons are sprayed on fields to control weeds, then ingested by animals, then excreted in manure. And even a few years later, that manure can destroy your garden. Trust me—I've been there. Unless you know that the farmer providing manure does not spray his fields or buy in hay from people that might, watch out! This stuff is nasty. If you have a choice between 10-10-10 and manure that might contain herbicides, go with the 10-10-10. Better to go chemical than to poison your garden beds for years to come.

Organic fertilizers are usually the healthiest choice for your soil long-term, but they can also be labor intensive, expensive, and a pain to deal with in larger farm situations. Ever try to make enough compost for a large garden? Ouch. There's never enough, unless you devote a lot of your garden to crops that make lots of biomass for the pile. In the case of growing things when the manure hits the fan, it's better to have lower-quality fertilizer and something to eat... than to stick to your organic roots and starve. I know—I'll get hate mail—but it's true.

Another benefit of chemical fertilizer: large amounts can be stored in small spaces. Fill a shed with bags of high-grade fertilizer and you've got the fertilizing equivalent of a massive barn filled with compost. Sure, it's not that great for your land long term, but that Big Shed O' Fertilizer might get you through to the other side of a collapse situation. Or it might get you raided by the Feds.

You: "It's for corn, officer, I *swear*!"

Officer: "Then how do you explain all these blasting caps?"

On the other hand, organic doesn't always have to be expensive, as we've seen with the case of urine. If a gardener was in a serious survival situation, he could have everyone pee into jugs for the duration and then feed his garden that way. No waste, no cost. It's not ideal, and it's rather horrifying to the faint of heart, but it's tried and true. Someone else tried it and told me about it. Yep, that's it.

A Little Post-Fight Commentary

You have to fertilize your plants with something, whichever route you choose. Now is the time to learn what works and what doesn't in your soil. Experiment. Stockpile when you can. I keep both chemical and organic fertilizers around, just in case, even though I grow almost all my produce organically. There may be a point where I have to farm a multiple-acre field to keep my family and friends fed, and I'll be darned if there's enough beer in the world to make the amount of pee needed for a plot that size.

There's plenty to think about when it comes to feeding your plants, so plan ahead now. There will be a time you need to feed yourself, and whether you go organic or chemical, you'll need to feed your plants and the soil first if you ever hope to create a sustainable food production plan.

If you really want to get deep into feeding your soil completely organically and with the least amount of work possible in a grid-down situation, I highly recommend you read my book on the subject: *Compost Everything: The Good Guide to Extreme Composting.*

Chapter 6

Pest Control

I pulled out the remains of summer's snake beans from one of my garden beds and was amazed by the sight that met my eyes: the roots were a horrid, knotty mass of distorted lumps.

Nematodes.

For those of you who don't know what nematodes are, be thankful. These particular pests are various microscopic members of the roundworm family that wreak havoc on plants.

In the spring my beans had done excellently, so I planted a second round in the same area. It grew rapidly but seemed to have a much harder time producing a crop than the earlier set of plants. In short, they were a fail.

Sometimes you can get away with planting an area multiple times in a row with the same crop. I have a neighbor who plants a plot of southern peas every summer. From what I can spy over the fence, it seems like they're in the same place. He seems to do fine; however, the plot probably reverts to weeds and grass through the rest of the year.

That time of rest can make all the difference.

Many of the problems in modern farming, from the need for extra pesticides to the use of genetically modified plants, relate to a lack of rotation. When the same ground is used to grow the same crops over and over again, pest problems start to build.

Granted, many farmers rotate between soybeans and corn or other pairings, but they don't have the luxury of putting space aside for long term rotation plans like a home gardener can do with his plots.

In the case of my knotted bean roots, I won't be planting anything susceptible to nematodes in that same space for a while, and I definitely won't be planting anything in the bean and pea family.

Instead, after pulling the beans, my wife and I cleaned up the bed. Then she sowed a good handful of mustard seeds across the surface of the nematode-ridden earth.

Mustard, like many of its brassica cousins, can actually repel nematodes. They hate eating mustard!

If you really want to improve a bed and kick out garden pests before they become a big issue, give your gardens even more time than a year or so between similar crops. In a small space this may not always be possible, but in a system like mine where I have a lot of beds it's pretty easy to pull off.

If you can rotate not just types, but entire plant families, you'll do well.

Hardcore Crop Rotation: A Five-Year Plan

If you really wanted to go nuts with your plant rotation, you could switch plant families for five years without many issues. Call it a five-year mission to boldly plant what no man has planted before.

When I was a kid, my brother and I used to bike over to my Grandma's house in the summer and watch *Star Trek* on her Beta VCR. We'd eat her amazing homemade macaroni and cheese - she used Vermont aged cheddar - along with frozen slices of mango from her tree out back. She also had air conditioning, and we didn't. It was awesome. Man, those were the days. No responsibilities, cool grandparents, fast bikes, Kirk and Spock, green ladies, a good brother to hang with... I must've watched 15,000 hours of *Star Trek* by the time I was 15.

Now where the heck was I? Ah yes, being a grownup and writing a book on gardening. You know, in retrospect, it's amazing I grew up to be thin, fit, handsome, and loving the outdoors... instead of being a huge bearded diabetic rolling around sci-fi conventions in a motor scooter trying to find an XXXL shirt with a picture of Captain Picard wearing a crown that reads something like *Resistance Is Feudal*.

Okay. Back to crop rotation. Try this five-year plan on for size:

Year 1
Spring: Snake beans / other beans (Fabaceae)
Fall: Mustard / Broccoli / Kale / Cauliflower (Brassicaceae)

Year 2
Spring: Corn / Rye / Wheat / Sorghum (Poaceae)
Fall: Carrots / Dill / Parsley / Cilantro (Apiaceae)

Year 3
Spring: Peppers / Tomatoes / Tobacco / Potatoes (Solanaceae)
Fall: Beets / Amaranth / Lettuce / Chard (Amaranthaceae)

Year 4
Spring: Sunflowers / Jerusalem Artichokes / Artichoke / Yacon (Asteraceae)
Fall: Garlic / Onions / Chives / Leeks (Amaryllidaceae)

Year 5
Spring: Squash / Cucumbers / Melons / Zucchini / Bitter Gourds (Cucurbitaceae)
Fall: Corn Salad (Caprifoliaceae)

If you really get all the way to corn salad, you're crazier than I am. I don't even know what that stuff is. Really, you don't have to go for a full five years: usually two is enough. However, this plan does give you an idea of how many crops from different families can be planted without repeating a family. There's some good food coming out of that bed, no matter what year you're in.

The Biblical Method of Crop Rotation

Exodus 23:10–11 states: 'For six years you shall sow your land and gather in its yield, but the seventh year you shall let it rest and lie fallow, that the poor of your people may eat; and what they leave the beasts of the field may eat. You shall do likewise with your vineyard, and with your olive orchard."

Basically, the land was left alone. With what we now know about tilling and the power of weeds to restore the soil this seems—shall we say—inspired?

It still works.

Some years ago I visited one of the University of Florida's agricultural research sites and was fascinated to see that they converted many of their test plots back to grass while they were between crop tests.

It makes sense when you consider that many insects and other garden pests are on multi-year cycles. If they nested in your corn one year, then were expecting to have corn again the next year and instead got boring old grass, they'd starve.

When the ground has a chance to just sit, it also rises in organic matter and nutrient content thanks to the working of fungi, bacteria, the rain, and the action of various weeds.

What about this for another addition to your crop rotation plans: add chickens!

I have an area of my front yard that was really lousy until I added a chicken tractor earlier this year. That ground greened up rapidly. As the chicken tractor denuded the ground and was moved from place to place, I chucked seeds all over the areas that had been tilled by the birds' relentless scratching for feed and insects. Chickens remove potential pests, adding manure, and seriously improving the soil as they go.

If you let animals eat the remains of previous gardens, as the Book of Exodus recommends, you're practicing an excellent method of land use rotation. The main reason to avoid repetition is to keep diseases and pests of one species from turning into plagues. Chickens can really bust that pest cycle to pieces.

Another Simple Solution

Here's another thing you can do if you're less of a long-term planner: mix your garden beds up.

When you plant in the spring, mix onions, carrots, lettuce, cabbage, garlic, peas, kale, etc. into the same bed, randomly arranged. No nice blocks! Then later in the year, you can plant in beans, tomatoes, squash, peppers, and other warm-season crops the same way.

With enough of a mix you'll have a lot of different flavors and scents that will confuse garden pests and keep the chances of seriously destructive disease within acceptable parameters.

Though it may not work for the neatnik, throwing a mix of seeds across a bed and thinning later can also work quite well.

Adding Additional Habitat for the Good Guys

Beyond mixing up your crops inside your garden beds, mixing up your homestead is a great idea as well.

Not so long ago, farmers preserved hedgerows between their fields. These sometimes consisted of deliberately planted trees or shrubs and sometimes consisted of wild trees and plants. Hazelnuts were a common choice, though often the patches were just little strips of native scrub brush between the plowed fields. Modern farming often plows a field from fence line to fence line, viewing these nature strips as a waste of space that could otherwise be turned to profit; however, newer studies are showing that hedgerows do a lot more than take up space.

Wild trees, plants, and weeds provide a place for birds to nest and for bees to build their hives. It's a place for snakes and toads, wasps and spiders, praying mantises and ladybugs. A hedgerow provides built-in pest control for your fields.

You can do this in a smaller way in your gardens. I've taken to planting mixed beds of perennial flowers, vegetables and small edible trees and shrubs right between my garden beds. One of these perennial patches might contain heirloom roses, perennial marigolds, a Japanese persimmon, chives, edible-leafed hibiscus, raspberries, and whatever little flowers my daughter wants to plant. It's a patch of dense and beautiful growth, always buzzing with insect life while providing an oasis for frogs and other bug-eaters.

If you don't feel like planting perennials in the middle of your gardening area, leave patches just outside your garden of native weeds and shrubs. Choose some areas, and quit mowing them. The good guys will move in. A messy ecosystem is a healthy ecosystem. There's nothing in nature that looks like rows of corn with bare dirt in between the stalks. It doesn't happen, and nature *hates* that sort of thing. She'll throw locusts and earworms and crows at you until you go mad. Yet, if you mix everything up into a more complete ecosystem, God's design of balance starts to kick in.

You don't want to lower the insect population; you want to raise it dramatically!

Look at what happens with deer when you remove the predators. Overpopulation quickly leads to denuded forests, landslides from erosion, and eventually, starving deer. But when there are plenty of hunters, wolves, or tigers, the deer population comes under control, and the remaining deer and forests are healthy. You don't want to kill all the deer, and you don't want to remove the predators, either.

Pests generally breed a lot faster than predators. They're also the first thing to find your garden. If you spray to kill the pests, you'll also knock out the predators in doing so. The pests precede the predators, meaning that just about the time they build up to plague proportions, there's almost always a predator that's going to appear and knock them down again.

The problem is, if you're growing a garden in a well-kept yard with few shrubs, flowers, weeds or other places for the good guys, it takes them a lot longer to find your garden and the pests inhabiting it. Pests are great at finding your plants regardless, but when there are places for the good guys to live, they'll be there when you need them.

One thing I've done to lower the caterpillar count in my yard is I've quit knocking out wasp nests. Wasps and hornets are caterpillar-killing machines. I've even seen them dragging dead grasshoppers around. You may hate getting stung, yet once you realize that wasps are trolling through your garden every day looking for caterpillars to kill, you start to go easy on the vicious little things. I've gone a step farther and added a row of mailboxes on the fence over my garden to give the wasps nice places to build their nests. I've also drilled lots of various-sized holes in chunks of wood and hung them in dry places where the solitary bees and wasps will find them and lay their eggs. For both pollination and insect control, wasps are awesome. Some of them even lay their eggs on caterpillars. When those eggs hatch, the hapless caterpillars are devoured inside out by tunneling wasp larvae. Disgusting but effective, and we need that kind of help in our gardens. I've even seen some sort of solitary bee stuffing dead stinkbugs into the wind chimes hanging on my back porch. Weird.

Another way to increase the beneficial population of insects and other predators is to add some sort of water feature to your gardening area. Ponds are particularly good, since they become a place where frogs and toads will breed and dragonflies and damselflies will lay their eggs. Passing bees and wasps will also sip the water between their job of pollinating and patrolling your garden.

I have to say I really have very few caterpillar issues any more, although they used to be terrible before I got wise to building a stronger garden ecosystem.

Just remember: habitat = free pest control. How cool is that?

Doing It Yourself

If you do end up with pest problems despite mixing up your crops and giving the predators places to live, you don't have to immediately buy something horrid to spray. Yes, I know it's fun to "kill bugs dead" with a stream of toxins; however, you don't really want to eat poison, do you? I don't. When everything collapses, you're also not going to have a big row of life-destroying chemicals to choose from at your garden center.

Going organic now makes sense, since organic pest control ideally shouldn't have to rely on much in the way of outside materials.

One really simple method to knock down pests is to make up some repellent sprays in your kitchen.

First, get a cup of lye, a cup of ammonia, 10 mothballs, some battery acid and a half-gallon of bleach, plus at least an ounce of Strontium-90 (this must remain submerged in kerosene until use, due to its reactivity with the air), and 2 teaspoons of salts of hydrocyanic acid, then...

That would be a joke.

All you really need to get rid of most insects is to put a couple of drops of dish soap in a spray bottle of water, then add in a few things they hate.

Here's one way to do it:

David The Good's Delicious Organic Aphid Spray Recipe

Materials:

- 2–3 garlic cloves
- 2–3 hot peppers
- Dish soap

- Spray bottle
- Coffee filter
- Quart jar or container

Gather together your garlic cloves and hot peppers. I like really hot ones such as cayenne, Thai, ghost, or habanero peppers. Aphids hate those.

Chop up the peppers with the garlic, and put them in a quart jar. Then fill the quart jar with boiling water.

Let steep overnight, then strain the liquid through a coffee filter into a spray bottle. Add two drops of dish soap to the mixture and shake it up.

Spray infested areas daily until they leave your garden.

Aphids hate the taste, the soap, the hot peppers, and the garlic, so they usually clear out or die quickly.

Generally, though, I ignore aphids. If they really bug me I blast them with the hose. I'm always cognizant of the fact that I may kill or drive off good ladybugs or other predators with my spraying. Unless it's a matter of life and death for the plant, I'm lax.

For a real killer insect spray, you can make a pest-smashing nicotine insecticide. Be careful with it, though. It really is poisonous.

David The Good's Totally Addicting Deadly Nicotine Spray Recipe

Materials:

- A generous handful of cigar butts

- An old pot
- Dish soap
- Spray bottle
- Coffee filter

First, take your old pot, throw in the cigar butts, and cover them with a quart or so of water. If you don't have cigar butts available, just buy a packet of rolling tobacco and use that. Chewing tobacco or pipe tobacco would likely work as well, though who knows what other weird stuff might be in chewing tobacco. Probably dead bugs and fiberglass.

Now set your pot to boiling. This will make your whole house smell like a wet ashtray. Some people may like this, though my wife doesn't for some reason. I like to cook the tobacco for an hour or so and let all the nicotine seep out. Then I let it sit overnight to steep even more.

After it's turned into scary black tobacco water, pour it through a coffee filter into a spray bottle (this requires a funnel), and add a few drops of dish soap.

Congratulations! You've made a viciously toxic insecticide! Don't leave it out where your kids can drink it or CIA agents can steal it for assassination attempts on unlikable dictators.

I made a couple of batches of this and went around spraying things to see what would happen. One group of aphids I sprayed on one of my grapevines as a test initially looked fine. When I came back the next day, they were still there—but they were dead! And blackened.

There are various other sprays you can make with vegetables oils, extracts, and essential oils but I haven't tried them. I don't even use the two sprays above anymore since I got wise to creating habitat around my gardens.

The Final Defense
That Should Probably Be the First Defense

The final thing that really keeps your garden pests from becoming a terror is you. If you plant your gardens near where you live, work, and play, you're going to see problems as they appear. If you make a point to walk the rows daily and keep a half an eye on your crops, things won't get out of control. Pest problems go from tiny to huge almost overnight. Watch, and you'll be able to nail them down before you lose a harvest.

When I notice stinkbug eggs glued on the leaves of a squash plant, I crush them. When I see a tiny hornworm on a tomato, I pick it off. When the aphids are sucking the life out of the new growth on my bean vines, I blast them off with the hose.

You can also walk around with a little container of soapy water. Any insect you knock into it will drown rapidly and bother your garden no more.

If you're not in the garden, you're going to miss problems that could have been stopped early on. Keep your eyes open, and keep your garden as close as you can.

Chapter 7

A Big Ol' Giant Crop List

If things collapse, you really only need a few solid crops to stay alive and kicking.

If I were to pick my top five annual vegetables for survival, I'd pick potatoes, sweet potatoes, winter squash, true yams (climate permitting—if it were a cold location I'd just add more potatoes), and cabbages. If I could choose five more after that, I'd add yard-long beans, turnips, cassava (climate permitting—where it freezes hard I'd grow Jerusalem artichokes instead), garlic, and kale.

If I could also throw in a few beds of tobacco, sugar cane, and a source of caffeine (whether it be tea, coffee, or a caffeine-rich holly like yerba mate or yaupon), life would be pretty good.

But beyond these major survival crops and a few indulgences, there are a lot of vegetables out there worth considering. Let's take a look at a bunch of them so this looks like a totally professional gardening book and people will say, "Hey look, he's got a big ol' giant crop list in there!"

Amaranth

One crop that I've grown for the last few years is amaranth. I also grow its close cousin *Celosia argentea* as a leaf crop, and cultivation details are the same. Amaranth is a relative of spinach and isn't a member of the grass family like most so-called grains. Its broad leaves are also edible, which gives it a multipurpose edge over most seed crops.

Originally, I grew amaranth as a chicken feed, then discovered my chickens weren't all that keen on it. Thanks, birdbrains. Then I wondered if it made sense to use it for porridges and such for my family, but the yields are less than exciting, though it was easier to deal with than a true cereal.

To harvest amaranth, you massage the mature flower heads and let the tiny seeds fall into whatever receptacle you have available. Take a trashcan lid, put a couple of holes in the lip, then tie a long piece of rope through it and loop that rope over the back of your neck with the lid facing bottom up, and position it like a tray in front of your waist, and you're all set to pick amaranth.

Once you've collected a batch of amaranth grains, you can put them in a big bowl with rounded edges and blow the bits of flower head out of the seeds. This is also a good time to pick out all the bugs. One unintended benefit of the amaranth in my backyard is that it attracts a lot of stinkbugs. So, being a good survivalist, I picked them out of the grain, swished them around in water to get them to blow out their stink glands, then fried and ate them with a bowl of amaranth porridge. There's a lot more protein in stinkbugs than in amaranth, though they weren't the best-tasting things in the world.

One other thing you need to know about amaranth: it self-seeds magnificently. One year I harvested a garden bed of amaranth, threw the spent stalks and heads to the goats, and the seeds have been popping up in that area ever since. Awesome.

Asparagus

Asparagus is one of the few perennial crops commonly grown in the United States. That means that it produces for more than just a year or two. It requires a well-dug bed and weeding. Mulch helps. Asparagus also takes a few years to yield good harvests. Asparagus root crowns are usually available in the late winter and early spring for planting. Give them some good compost and mulch, plus some yearly amendments, and you'll be eating well in the apocalypse. I wouldn't count on them as any kind of a survival crop, but they are an excellent vegetable and quite nutritious. In some states asparagus grows wild. Learn to identify it, and you won't even have to grow your own.

Beans (Bush, Pole, Yard-long, and Southern Peas)

Beans are a must-have crop that comes in a wide variety of types. My two favorite types are bush green beans and snake beans for completely different reasons.

Green beans are one of the most basic vegetables you can grow. Reliable, productive, tolerant of poor soil and tasty, they are one of the first crops any new gardener should try.

Of course, there are many beans that fall into the "green bean" category. If it's called a "green bean," that basically just means it's a bean with an edible pod you eat while the beans are still unripe. If it's a variety you let hang on the plant until the beans are basically ripe, it's a "shell bean." Some varieties of shell beans are eaten while still soft, others are allowed to dry completely until you have "dry beans."

Beyond the "shell" or "green" varieties, beans also come in "bush" and "pole" varieties. Bush beans are usually small, squat plants that can stand without support. Pole beans are climbers and need trellises to do well. Bush green beans are drop-dead easy. No trellises, no drying, no shelling. Plus, quite a few can be grown in a small space.

When I was six I went to the store with Dad to buy some seeds. The yellow beans caught my eye, we bought them, and they went into my very first garden. They were Burpee's Brittle Wax beans. I'm still growing them today because they're consistent, productive, and taste good. They're not the most flavorful bean we grow, but they look cool, and they remind me of my great childhood garden.

Another favorite of mine is the Purple Romano bean. The purple color makes them really easy to see and pick off the plants, even though they turn green when cooked.

Beyond varieties, let's talk about culture. Beans like warm weather and will not stand freezing temperatures. Bush beans do not have the strong root system of pole beans, so they need a bit more water to stay happy. Plant your beans 1 inch deep and about 6 inches apart in rows roughly 12 inches apart, and you'll do fine. In a week or less, they'll pop up, and it's off to the races.

Beans usually start producing pods in less than two months. Once pods start getting to picking size, keep them picked. If you don't, the plant will give up producing new pods.

Bush beans can be sown multiple times through the warm season, and you'll get more beans that way. Plant a new bed every three weeks or so, and you'll be rolling in tasty pods.

As for pests, you'll get stink bugs and maybe bean beetles later as the summer progresses. I don't worry about them unless we get a total plague. One year the bean beetles totally chewed through a bed I'd planted. Fortunately, we'd already harvested plenty of beans. It was my own fault they went nuts, though. I had planted the bean bed in a monoculture of nice, even rows for the beetles to feast upon. Nothing but beans for miles, man.

If you get problems like that, I'd just bury the plants under some other crop area, bugs and all, wait a bit, and start over again. Or burn them. Or chuck them over the fence for your chickens to mangle. No big deal. Seed is cheap, and beans grow fast. Beans are also a nitrogen-fixer, so planting them in front of demanding crops and on new ground is a great way to give your garden a boost of fertility. I throw beans into empty corners during the warm season, just as I do with peas during the cool season. They're tough enough to thrive without much care... and they feed the ground. All aboard the bean train!

But the best thing about green beans? Letting your kids eat them right out of the garden, sweet and sun-warmed. When I pick a basket, I always acquire little "helpers" who wish to eat the beans. And since the pods are pesticide-free, nutritious, and abundant... who am I to say no?

Now let's talk about snake beans: *Vigna unguiculata*, also called the Yard-long Bean, the Snake Bean, the Asparagus Bean, and various other weird names, is an Asian green bean that kicks tail in humid or hot climates. I mean, *serious* tail. This thing is a monster.

The pods aren't really a yard long, though they are quite impressive at roughly a cubit. (Yeah, I said cubit. It's a legitimate unit of measure. Look it up.)

Let's talk about how crazy awesome these babies are.

The vines grow really long with little or no care. If you grow these, which you should, make sure you've got plenty of climbing room for them. Something fascinating about this plant: you can basically plant it at any warm time of the year as long as you give it enough water to get started. I planted them in mid summer and got a good crop, as well as in fall and spring. This sucker grows like a weed. I've even stuck seeds in the front yard and let them run across the grass and eat neighboring trees and shrubs. With zero care, they still bore beans. I once planted them in a spot that received only indirect light: they bore a large crop anyhow. Another time I planted them on a baking-hot fence. Same deal. Tons of beans.

And what beans! The taste is almost nutty. A lot of green bean flavor with overtones of roasted almond and a bit of asparagus.

Snake beans take a little while to get started. For a few weeks, they're just cute little bean plants. And then they pull the Incredible Hulk routine on you and start reaching for the sky in a blinding green rush.

The seeds are available rather widely now in a variety of cultivars. Every one I've grown has been vigorous and productive, though the purple types were less tasty than the green ones. My guess is that snake beans are just one step removed from weeds and have had little of their vitality bred out by successive genetic manipulation. Bugs leave them alone for the most part, and the vines are really good at climbing on whatever is handy. They also respond well to diluted urine as a fertilizer. Mix it 6:1 or so with water and spray it on the leaves.

Also, this plant is a nitrogen fixer and a good source for compost at year's end. It has no tolerance for frost, however, so don't plant it too close to frost dates.

The beans can be eaten raw or cooked and continue bearing for a few months after maturity. Pick the pods before they get too big and leathery. You'll get a feel for it quickly when you grow them. Just a few beans are enough for a good serving at dinner. And in case I didn't mention it: they're delicious.

Beets

Beets are nutrient-dense and not all that hard to grow, provided you give them decent soil and enough water. Plant them about 2–3 months before the expected first frost date for a fall crop, or plant your first round of beets a few weeks before the last spring frost date for a crop in the spring. Beet seeds don't like to germinate when temperatures are below 50 degrees Fahrenheit, so keep that in mind. If it's too cold, they may rot in the ground or fail to emerge until later.

Beets take about two months to start being of a harvestable size and sometimes longer. The greens are also edible, though when eaten raw they can sometimes make your throat scratchy.

One cool trick is to cut open a beet and get the juice on yourself. This makes people think you're bleeding and is loads of fun at parties, weddings, and other social occasions.

Broccoli

I used to think there was some magic to growing broccoli. It was a strange and beautiful plant I didn't feel comfortable trying. I don't know why, but somehow beans, cucumbers, beans, radishes, and more beans were less scary to me than broccoli. Anything but broccoli.

That all changed the fateful year my wife decided she wanted to try growing broccoli. Since I am benevolent, I figured I'd let her try and see what happened. What happened was amazing—we had lots of delicious broccoli. Perfect heads. Lush greens. Amazing flavor. And since then, we've grown plenty more, starting them from seeds in the spring and fall.

So what was the trick to growing broccoli?

Letting my wife do it!

In reality, I believe we have great luck with broccoli because we keep it well-watered, well-fertilized, and also mixed in with other crops like peas, carrots, and beets, making it less attractive to pests. I'm also a firm believer in foliar feeding with compost tea or fish emulsion. I've seen sad-looking plants turn into green giants after a few applications.

Though they're usually grown for their cluster of flower buds, broccoli leaves are also edible in salads (although you might want to remove the tough mid-ribs first), or as a cooked green. The flavor is very similar to that of collards, which makes sense, since collards are its less blue-blood relative.

It's often the case that a garden plant with one edible part also has other portions that can be eaten. Take sweet potatoes and their edible leaves, for example. Those extra uses are just icing. Or salads, as the case may be. Which are generally better for you than icing.

As a survival crop, broccoli isn't the easiest or most productive thing to grow. It likes decent soil and good care. It's also recognizable as food. On the up side, broccoli is delicious, healthy, and can grow through a mild winter without being troubled by frost. Further north you'll want to grow it outside of winter, however, since the plants will die if temperatures get too low or freeze hard for too long.

When you harvest broccoli, just cut the first big head off before it gets close to blooming. Then keep checking on the plant; it's going to grow multiple side shoots that will make many smaller heads as they grow. Keep cutting! Once that baby goes to seed, you're done. The harvest season can be really long with broccoli.

In my experience, broccoli does best right from seed, rather than as a transplant. Forget the expensive transplants. Buy a pack of seeds and scatter away, then thin 'em out and eat the thinnings.

If you've got a space for luxury foods, put in broccoli. At the very least, it may serve to keep some members of the Bush family out of your garden.

Brussels Sprouts

Brussels sprouts are a somewhat touchy crop, and I don't recommend them for a survival garden unless you have a long cool season and good soil.

Buckwheat

Buckwheat isn't a true grain, but its seeds are healthful and tasty, particularly if you like to eat a lot of pancakes.

Plant buckwheat in the spring after the last frost date. It will take so-so soil, but if you have better ground and more fertility, you'll get more of a harvest.

When the seed heads on buckwheat start darkening up, you can cut the entire plant and hang it up to dry. Later you can winnow out the seeds.

I confess: I don't usually go through the trouble of harvesting buckwheat for the table. I just grow it as a "green manure" crop I can till under to add organic matter to the soil. When most of the seeds look ready to harvest, I go around pulling clusters of them off while leaving the stems and roots of the plant still in the soil. Later I cut and drop the plants as mulch or till them into the ground.

Whatever seeds fall from buckwheat will rapidly sprout and grow another crop, so know that before you plant. It likes to come back! Fortunately, the plants are easy to pull out if you decide you've had enough buckwheat.

Buckwheat creates seeds very quickly so you can grow multiple crops a year. I buy raw buckwheat grain from the local organic market in their bulk bins, then use that to plant beds.

Cabbage

Cabbage is healthy, grows with moderate ease, and is storable for a decent amount of time under refrigeration or in a root cellar. If you ferment it, it stores even better. Sauerkraut fueled Germany for untold centuries, and its cousin kimchi is a Korean staple. Live fermented cabbage is incredibly healthy: it can fix stomach complaints, provide you with a lot of bio-available nutrition, and make your house smell amazing.

Cabbage is a cool-season crop that can be grown in early spring, and often again in the fall, depending on your climate. Red varieties are very nutritious, but the green types aren't slackers in healthiness, and they're bigger and usually sweeter. I grow cabbage from seed, but I make sure to give them enough space to grow. Seed planted about every 4 to 6 inches, and rows 2 feet apart works for me. I thin the cabbages to 2 feet apart as they grow, so that they don't have to fight for nutrients and can spread out. Eat the baby plants in salads, or right from the garden. Delicious.

Down south, you should probably stick to small-headed varieties that can take the growing heat of spring. Up north you can grow the massive types and make barrels of sauerkraut.

Cabbage is one of my must have crops: it is good fresh as a snack, made into coleslaw, stir-fried, and of course, sauerkraut. I really like sauerkraut. Now, if I can just get my bratwurst tree to take off!

Carrots

The biggest pain with carrots is their tiny seeds and inconsistent germination. Once you get past that, they're pretty easy to grow. They're a cool season crop that can take a little frost. I plant them in early spring by making shallow furrows a foot apart in a well-raked seedbed, then sprinkling the tiny seeds generously in the furrows, followed by a sprinkling of soil or compost on top. Keep watered (but don't spray them too hard!) for a couple of weeks, and soon little green carrot shoots will start to emerge.

About a week after they come up, I start thinning them out with a pair of scissors. I simply snip stems off at soil level until I've thinned them to 1 inch apart. A few weeks later, I will go back and then snip them to two inches apart and let them grow up from there.

You can tell how big your carrots are by gently brushing the soil away from the tops. When the diameter hits at least an inch, I start pulling them.

Carrot greens are also edible and have a flavor quite similar to their cousin, parsley.

Cassava

Most people have no idea what cassava is even though it's eaten throughout many of the equatorial nations of the world. If you've ever eaten tapioca pudding, you've eaten cassava. Cassava is primarily a root crop, though the leaves are also edible when well-cooked.

Cassava plants are tall, graceful and tropical in appearance. I've had them grow up to 12 feet! Its palmate leaves are attractive in the landscape or the garden. The Latin name is *Manihot esculenta*, but it's known commonly as manioc, tapioca plant, or yuca (not to be confused with yucca, despite what spell-checker says. Yucca is a completely different plant).

Whatever you call it, cassava is a serious staple crop. Virtually pest free, drought tolerant, loaded with calories, capable of good growth in poor soil—cassava is a must-have any place it can grow.

Additionally, cassava is much less work than growing grain, and it's very forgiving when it comes to harvest time. In fact, once it has hit maturity, you can basically dig roots at any point for a few years, though sometimes older roots may become too woody to eat.

That said, if temperatures drop to freezing for any period of time, your cassava will freeze to the ground. This won't usually kill the plant so long as the ground doesn't freeze, but it does mean you need to plan your growing accordingly. I mulch over the roots in fall to ensure they survive.

In the tropics, cassava will live for years. The plant never dies back unless you live north of USDA growing zone 10, then occasional frosts will knock it down. Growing it in any zone colder than Zone 8 is probably futile unless you have a big greenhouse. Cassava needs plenty of warm days and nights to make big roots.

Unlike most garden crops, cassava is not grown from seeds except perhaps for breeding purposes. The only way you're going to grow it is via stem cuttings. Roots purchased from an ethnic market are very unlikely to work since they lack growing buds. You need fresh cuttings to get them going.

To grow from cuttings, chop a sturdy stem into pieces at least a foot long (I prefer a bit longer), then stick them right side up half-way into the ground. You can also lay them on their sides in a 2–4 inch trench and cover them with soil. Multiple shoots will pop up in a few weeks, provided it's nice and warm outside.

Root development takes 6–12 months, depending on water, soil, temperature, and growing conditions. Where it freezes, harvestable roots can take 18 months or more to develop due to the complete lack of growth during the cold of winter and the need for the plant to regrow a healthy top in the spring.

To harvest, I machete down the entire plant a foot or so from the ground, throw the branches to the side and start digging. Be careful, though—the roots are easy to chop through. Some careful exploratory digging with your hands or a trowel is recommended. The roots you're looking for grow down and away from the main stem and are generally located in the first 2 feet of soil. They're deep brown with flaky skin. Don't dig roots more than a few days before you're going to eat them because cassava stores quite poorly once disconnected from the mother plant.

Once you've harvested the roots, you can use the rest of the plant to make a new set of cuttings for planting. I snap off all the leaves and compost them, then cut the bare canes into planting size. Canes that are too green and young tend to rot rather than root, so through them on the compost as well. Sturdy 1–2-inch diameter canes are perfect.

When you plant, ensure they're right side up by looking for the tiny little growth buds by the leaf bases (or where the leaves were before they hit the compost bin). That little dot should be above the leaf's base, not below.

To keep cassava cuttings for spring in an area prone to frost, bury cut canes in a box beneath the ground through the winter. I've also dug a hole, filled it with cut canes, covered the canes with straw and thrown a tarp over the whole thing. Alternately, you can simply start some cane cuttings in pots and bring them in on frosty nights.

The way you prepare cassava for eating is important since the roots are *toxic when raw*. To get cassava ready for the table, gather up your harvested roots and wash them. Then slit and remove the outer peels on the roots. This layer usually comes off pretty easily. In the middle of the root is a thread of woody core that can be removed by halving or quartering the roots and peeling or cutting it out.

Now that you have cleaned cassava roots, just boil them until soft and they'll be safe to eat. If you can push a fork into a piece easily, it's done. At that point, you can serve the roots... or, do one better and towel them off and fry them. That tastes much better than boiled roots. Cassava is a good addition to stews, soups, curries, Crock-Pot recipes, and more. Treat it like a dense, slightly sweet potato.

Cauliflower

Cauliflower grows much like broccoli. Treat it the same way, and you'll do fine.

Chaya

Chaya, also known as Mexican tree spinach, is in the same wild, wonderful, beautiful, and often toxic family as cassava. It also contains some cyanide, so you need to take care not to eat it raw, even if you want to. Just don't. Stop. Put it down. *No!*

Boil leaves for 20 minutes, then enjoy them. They're ridiculously good for you and full of vitamins, which makes sense to me since they taste hearty and delicious.

Growing chaya is a cinch if you can find cuttings and if you live in a relatively frost-free area. If not, they'll freeze to the ground and come back in the spring unless the ground freezes or you get a long period of cold.

Cuttings root in a month or so when it's warm. Just stick them in moist soil and wait. They're not as fast as cassava, but they'll usually take. Once you get a couple of plants, it's easy to make more.

Bugs don't seem to bother my chaya plants, presumably due to the cyanide content, and they grow decently even in poor soil. I've planted them in full sun and in almost full shade, and they've lived in both places, though the ones grown in shade are thin and leggy.

Grab some chaya, tuck a few into your yard... and you'll have great perennial greens for years to come. This plant's a winner.

Collards

Collards are an under-appreciated staple of the Deep South. The thing that really makes collards great is their long season of production. Most other crops get toasted by frost... but these guys will take cold down into the teens. In USDA zone 8 and southward, you can grow them right through the entire winter and they'll sometimes survive through a winter north of there!

Out of the brassica family, collards are right up there with radishes on the "ease of growing" scale. They're tough, take the cold, grow and grow and grow, and rarely if ever will fail to give you a harvest.

Other bonuses to collards: young leaves are excellent in salads. Cooked and cut into strips, they can fill in for pasta in low-carb diets. My wife makes a killer paleo "collard lasagna."

To plant the easy way, prepare a bare patch of ground, then scatter seeds, rake them around, and water for a week. Baby plants will come up everywhere. Thin as needed to give them space for growth, and eat the thinnings. Harvest leaves as needed. The plants will take a lot of cutting.

And seriously, if you're not growing these yet, set aside a patch for spring or fall: collards are a must-have.

Corn

I like corn because the grains look cool. Obviously, since I've noticed that, it makes me completely superficial. Other grains don't look like jewels when they're threshed, hulled, cleaned, or whatever you need to do to them to get them ready for eating. Corn, however, is in a class of its own.

The corn I'm talking about, of course, is grain corn, not sweet corn. Sweet corn is for fun: grain corn is for survival.

Unfortunately, corn has become a byword for the evils of modern agriculture. The plant has been used to make evil high-fructose corn syrup and had its genes scrambled into genetically modified variants that can stand being sprayed with poisons that would put us into a coma.

Corn is also a greedy crop that likes a lot of fertilizer as well as disturbed soil. When you grow it conventionally, you end up with erosion, run off, etc. In another negative, corn, when used as a staple (and not nixtamalized, which is a form of processing that uses lime to make corn's nutrients bioavailable), is also linked to pellagra, a niacin deficiency that can make you go nuts and try to write gardening books for a living.

But!

Corn also has a lot of positives going for it other than having kernels that look cool. It is:

1. Easy to grow
2. Productive
3. Easy to clean and utilize

4. Storable
5. Calorie dense
6. A good biomass producer
7. Great for chicken feed
8. Delicious

Sometimes extended rains will ruin some of your crop around harvest time... sometimes the bugs take over... and sometimes a nasty blast of wind will blow all your stalks sideways. Yet even with those drawbacks, it's usually simple to grow. Over the last few years, I've tested five different varieties in North Central Florida and a few more in the tropics.

Save yourself some trouble and know this: if you're growing corn in Yankee territory or any temperate area, flint types are your best bet. If you're growing in the Confederate states or anywhere with a long, hot summer, dent corns are what you need.

Three years ago we had a great stand of Hickory King (an old heirloom) dent corn that produced excellently on tilled soil amended with cow manure. Two years after I planted Tex Cuban (a more modern breed selected for the tropics) on tilled soil and fertilized it with chicken manure tea, and it did quite well. The ears weren't as large as the Hickory King ears, but that may be the result of genetic depression or lower soil fertility in the plot. It's hard to tell when you don't grow things side-by-side in the same season. Since then, I have been unable to find Tex Cuban again so I am back to growing the tastier Hickory King variety.

All that stuff aside, grain corn is a lot easier to grow than sweet corn. It's more tolerant of temperature fluctuations and pests as well as lower soil fertility.

The first time I ground grits from kernels harvested from my own garden, I was blown away by the rich corn flavor of homegrown heirlooms. There's nothing like it.

If you pick grain corns in the "milk stage"—that is, about the level of maturity at which you'd pick a sweet corn—they make a good, full-flavored corn-on-the-cob. On the island of Grenada you can buy roasted grain corn at roadside stands, as its a popular street food. In the mature stage, other than grits, you can turn the kernels into cakes, chips, tortillas, cornbread, and other delicacies.

To grind the corn into meal or grits, a Corona grain mill works fine. For finer grinds, though, you might need to get a better grinder. I bought a Country Living Grain Mill which is supposed to grind corn (I have the right auger for it), yet it refused to do a decent job for me, perhaps because the relative humidity was too high or something stupid like that. A cheap Corona-type grain mill can be bought in any Mexican grocery, and I find that running the corn through one of those a couple of times is good enough.

Corn makes for great chicken feed if you "crack" it roughly in your mill so the birds can eat it. Whole kernels can be handled by larger birds, but I'd rather give them easier-to-handle sizes.

Also, if you are growing your own tobacco (more on that later), corn cobs make great pipes to smoke it in. Who needs fancy imported briar from some fruity European nation? If corn cobs were good enough for General MacArthur, they're more than good enough for me. I've made my own pipes from various materials and can attest to the fact that nothing tastes as pleasant as a corn cob.

A final note on corn: the stalks are great forage for grazing animals, as well as being a good addition to the compost pile. I stack them on the bottom of a new pile to add air, then pile smaller stuff on top. By spring you'll have plenty of compost to feed the next crop of corn.

If you haven't tried growing grain corn, give it a go. You might fall in love at first glance, just as I did.

Cucumbers

Cucumbers can be really easy or not easy at all, depending on the bugs, your climate, your soil fertility, and which variety you choose to plant. I've had the best luck with pickling types, which are smaller and bumpier cukes; however, I've seen other gardeners swear by the big Oriental types or tell me how wonderfully their 'Straight 8" cucumbers do.

To grow cucumbers, make sure you add some good fertilizer and/or compost to the planting area and give them a good trellis to climb. Plant in the spring after the last frost date in full sun and warm soil. When they start making cucumbers about two months after emerging, keep the plants picked regularly for maximum yields. If the cucumbers get blimp-sized and start to turn yellow, you've waited too long to harvest.

Keep an eye out for stink bugs and other pests. Everything seems to like eating cucumbers.

Eggplant

Eggplant? Seriously... you want to eat eggplant while the world is collapsing around you?

Okaaaaay, though it sounds pretty decadent to me. Should we be eating more potatoes or something?

Plant seeds or transplants in the garden after the last frost date. Give them lots of good compost or a balanced fertilizer, then watch out for insects. Eggplants, like their cousins tomatoes and peppers, cannot handle the frost. Keep them picked, and they'll often produce quite well over a long period.

Fava Beans

Fava beans are the only bean you can grow in the winter. They take temperatures down into the teens, but if you get that cold regularly, you'll probably want to grow them as a spring or fall crop instead of all the way through.

Plant fava beans a few weeks before your last frost date in the spring or in the fall once temperatures have cooled down. They don't really like the heat.

Fava beans make a good green manure crop (more on that in my book *Compost Everything*) since they fix nitrogen and create large-sized tender plants that compost easily and rot quickly when tilled under.

To harvest, pick the pods when the beans fill out nicely inside, then shell them and cook for the table.

Garlic

Garlic, although not what one might consider a major crop, is healthy, easy to grow, calorie dense, space efficient, and makes life better. It stores well, can be pickled, and is hardy enough to withstand quite a bit of freezing. In Tennessee, I planted it in the fall, and it would sit through most of the winter, and burst into growth in the spring. We ate a lot of garlic, and it tasted much better than anything you would get in the store.

In colder climates, you may have to just plant it in the early spring. If you want to save garlic to plant again the next year, save complete heads, as they keep a lot better than individual cloves.

When you plant garlic, you can get pretty dense in the planting spaces; I plant cloves 2 to 4 inches deep, in 6-inch squares. This makes for a lot of garlic in early summer.

You know it is time to harvest when the tops turn yellow and die down. Carefully pull the heads, and hang them some place out of the weather to dry out.

If you're really clever, you can braid the tops together. I'm not really clever; I just let them dry for a while, then store them in baskets. You also might want to check with your local agricultural extension to see which varieties are recommended for your area. There are hard-neck, soft-neck, and everything in between. Check it out, and find out what works in your area.

Beyond its culinary value, garlic is also a good antibiotic, as well as being a pest and vampire repellent.

Ginger

Ginger is a tropical root that can be grown in pots or in the garden, providing your climate allows. If you live north of USDA zone 8, grow ginger in pots; if you're south of zone 8, grow it in the ground.

Ginger is propagated from roots, not seeds. Over the years, I've planted ginger root from the store many times; however, good roots are getting harder to find. A lot of what I've seen lately is limp stuff from China without any good "eyes" on it. You have to look hard to get good pieces.

You want roots that have eyes that look like nice, healthy, yellow-green bumps. Those are where your new ginger plants will grow from.

When you have your nice, healthy pieces of ginger, break them up into a few pieces if they're huge chunks, and ensure each piece has at least one or two growing buds.

Bury them about 4–6 inches deep and wait. In a few months, ginger plants will pop up in a lovely row, and it's off to the races.

Ginger is a perennial plant, not an annual, so once you have a patch, you'll have it for years. Unlike most garden vegetables, however, ginger hates direct sunlight. Only plant it in the shade. If you have a piece of your yard that doesn't get enough sun for regular veggies, plant it with ginger.

Ginger goes dormant in the winter, dying back to the ground. This doesn't mean it's dead. Just wait, it'll come back in late spring unless you have really cold winters. It's gotten down to 12 degrees overnight at my homestead, and my ginger has still come back without any problems. If you are growing in pots, just bring your pots in for the winter.

After your ginger plants have been in the ground for a year, you can pull a little bit of roots; however, I find that the best harvests come at the two year mark and beyond. Dig around the base of the plant when it dies back in the fall or winter and take what you need—just make sure you leave some pieces there to grow back the next spring.

We use ginger for seasoning (the leaves can be added to soups like bay leaves) and to treat upset stomachs. Shredded, chunked, or powdered—roots also add extra flavor to soup bases.

Grains

Grain: the staff of life. We've heard that before. And it's true. Much of the world uses one grain or another as their staple crop. Wheat is popular in much of the temperate world, rice reigns across much of Southeast Asia, barley is vitally important as the main grain for brewing, and corn is king over all.

Beyond these, rye and oats are both of high importance worldwide, and to a lesser extent, minor grains like millet and sorghum, plus pseudocereals like buckwheat, amaranth, and quinoa fill key food roles in some cultures.

Yield-wise, however, most grains aren't all that impressive. If you wanted to feed yourself on a small acreage, you probably wouldn't plant wheat, rye, oats, or barley. Not only are they cheap to purchase at the moment, these grasses are also out-yielded by potatoes and other root crops.

I sometimes grow barley, wheat, and oats through the fall and spring... yet I rarely eat what I grow. The chickens get the stalks, seed heads and all, as bedding. Sometimes the kids and I pick through a few but usually don't bother. The work is murder. Yet, fortunately, not all grains are like that.

The only grain I think makes sense on a small scale is corn, which I covered above. A good-sized patch of grain corn will produce a decent amount of kernels for grits, cornbread, flour, chicken feed, etc. And of course, the yield of that space skyrockets when you intercrop by adding squash and beans to the mix. That's something you can't easily do with other grains.

Grains can be a part of your small homestead, certainly. Some will even provide you with moderate yields. However, if I were in a situation where I needed high-yield in a small space,

I'd look elsewhere. Cabbages, collards, turnips, potatoes, carrots, beets, pole beans, Jerusalem artichokes, winged yams, and heck, even okra, will out-yield grains.

That doesn't mean they're not worth trying or using as cover crops. There are grains that will keep the ground covered during winter. There are grains that will produce valuable food for your animals and matter for your compost pile. There are even grains that make great Thanksgiving decorations—just don't count on them to be your staple in a crisis unless you're willing to work like a slave.

Jerusalem Artichokes

Jerusalem artichokes are a native North American root crop and a member of the sunflower family. They're remarkably productive, though they also give you incredible intestinal discomfort if you're not used to eating them. You could likely use them as a source of natural gas in a crisis, though the logistics of capturing said gas would be problematic.

I planted buckets of Jerusalem artichokes in my yard in Tennessee. I started with a handful of tubers a friend gave me in early spring, planted those, then watched as they grew into magnificent plants and burst into glorious bloom in the fall. After the frosts took the above-ground growth, I dug down to find many, many pounds of tubers beneath the clay. I harvested a big pile of them in the spring and planted them with the help of my four-year-old daughter. I'd dig a little hole, she'd toss in a tuber, I'd dig a hole, she'd toss in a tuber, then after doing this over about 400 square feet of the backyard by a drainage ditch, we filled in all the holes and called it a day.

By the middle of next summer, the area was a forest of Jerusalem artichokes and the view of the ditch was completely obscured by a lush wall of green.

That fall, I dug up a terrifying number of tubers. This was amazing to me. I never watered those things, never sprayed for bugs, never weeded and never even prepared the soil other than hacking little holes through the grass when we planted. Some were even growing in rocky clay that had been torn up by construction equipment and inverted so the topsoil was basically gone. One part of the patch was even in the shade, and it produced some, though not nearly as much as the sunny areas did.

Jerusalem artichokes are survivors—and if you grow them, you will be too. They are a perennial that does better if you harvest regularly. People like to say "watch out—those things are invasive!"

And that's exactly what you want as a survival gardener. Food that takes care of itself. Just don't plant them in the middle of your lettuce bed. Plant them at the edge of your garden where they can grow year after year. When you harvest, you're bound to leave some tubers in the ground and get more Jerusalem artichokes returning the next year. It's an in-ground caloric food bank.

To grow your own Jerusalem artichokes, plant tubers a few inches deep in the fall, winter, or early spring, and don't forget where you planted them. It's easy to miss the first flush of growth amidst the weeds that pop up in spring, so be easy with that lawnmower or tiller!

Once the plants are taller, they'll rapidly out-compete everything around them. They'll grow all summer and get up to 12 feet tall, then burst into glorious bloom around October. The flowers look like miniature sunflowers and are good as a cut flower.

You can dig Jerusalem artichokes in the fall after the tops of the plants die and then harvest right on through the winter, provided your ground isn't frozen solid. The roots are formed in a big clump at the base of the main stalk later in the year. This clump is usually about 2 feet across and consists of a bunch of lumpy little tubers all jammed together. I like to pick out the big ones for the table and re-plant the little ones. You can keep harvesting into the spring until things start to warm up. The tubers rapidly deteriorate in the spring as their stored energy is expended in pushing up new Jerusalem artichoke plants.

Jerusalem artichokes are edible raw or cooked—just be careful not to eat many until you know what your digestive tract is going to do with them. Add them to your diet a little at a time. The flavor is mild, crunchy and sweet, similar to carrots but less strongly flavored.

This is a plant for surviving a complete crash. So get them in the ground as soon as you can. If you really can't stand them, feed them to your livestock and then eat the livestock.

Kale

Kale is both a healthy green and good medicine. There are reports of kale helping reverse the progression of multiple sclerosis, lower cholesterol, improve eyesight, and fight cancer. Kale is believed to contain the most nutrition per calorie of any known terrestrial plant.

When the Flintstone vitamins run out, kale will be there for you.

Kale is an easy-to-grow cool-season biennial. It thrives on double-dug beds, even in sand, and can produce for more than half the year. Plant kale in fall or early spring, taking care not to bury the tiny seeds too deep. One kale plant (depending on variety) can easily grow a couple of feet tall and spread to the same extent. I over-seed, then eat what I thin out. Give them enough water when they're little, and they'll reward you with plenty of growth.

Unlike tomatoes and other warm-season crops, kale isn't fazed by frosts. The taste gets even sweeter after a frost. In the south, kale grows all the way through the winter; farther north its growth may slow or stop if it's cold. If you get below the teens, kale may get killed in the cold. If you're a gourmet, consider growing the attractive *Lacinato*, or "Dinosaur" kale. If you live farther north, consider Russian or Siberian varieties known to survive extreme cold.

The only time it's difficult to grow kale is during the heat of summer. High temperatures are kale's enemy. The season could likely be expanded if you grow it under grape trellises or taller crops so it's protected from the worst of the sun's heat.

If you grow kale, you could be eating fresh greens even when there's snow covering the garden. Just dig down and take what you need.

Kohlrabi

Kohlrabi is fun to grow just because it looks cool. Imagine a green Sputnik, and you have an idea what kohlrabi looks like.

It tastes like a mild broccoli and grows at the same time of the year. Give it a little attention, some good soil, and enough water, and you'll do well.

Lettuce

Lettuce isn't as nutritious at most of the greens on this list, but it does make a really nice salad ingredient. Loose-leaf types are usually easier to grow than head types. Every spring we plant some lettuce mixes in the garden and enjoy everything from the pale yellowy-green Black Seeded Simpson to the rich red and green cultivars. Mix in mild lettuces with stronger-flavored greens such as kale in order to make a salad that balances taste and nutrition. Though lettuce is a cool season crop, it doesn't really like frost. Plant early in the spring or at the beginning of the fall. Lettuce will turn bitter and go to seed if it gets hot. It's also thrifty on space and can be grown easily in pots.

Melons

Whether or not you have success with melons really depends on your climate, your experience, and the varieties you grow. Watermelons have done much better for me than cantaloupes or canary melons down here in the south; however, your mileage may vary. Ask local gardeners how they grow their melons and what varieties have done well for them.

Melons like good soil and lots of room to roam. In cooler climates, some gardeners will plant them in a mound surrounded by black plastic since they like the heat and because the plastic acts as a weed block.

Plant a few melon seeds on a mound of compost in the spring, and they'll love you for it. Make sure it's well after the last expected frost date, however. Melons love the heat and hate the cold.

Moringa

Moringa has been called the "Miracle Tree," and for good reason. From cleaning water to fending off malnutrition, it's a tree of many uses. Fast-growing, easy to grow, and containing complete proteins in its leaves, Moringa is a must-have for survival gardeners in warm climates. The leaves are absolutely loaded with nutrients, brought up from deep down by the tree's questing roots. The tree has been named the "most nutritious on earth."

Moringa is also anti-bacterial and anti-fungal, as well as being a really fast producer of biomass. Its pods are often called "drumsticks" and feature prominently in some regions of South Asia, however, it's sometimes hard to get them to set pods in regions with frost.

From seed, Moringa will easily hit 10 feet during its first year of growth. In the tropics the tree is alleged to reach 60 feet, though the wood is very weak. In our experience near the equator we never saw one more than twenty-five feet. Some of my moringa trees blew through 20 feet in their second year in North Florida, despite winter freezes.

But tall trees aren't really what you want. You want trees that are easy to harvest. To get that, simply cut the trunks at about 4 feet, and let them shoot up lots of tender new growth.

The compound leaf stems are easy to break off so the tiny leaflets can be dropped into soups, sprinkled into salads or dried/frozen for future use. After learning of its incredible nutrient profile, I started putting the leaves into everything from smoothies to scrambled eggs. Bonus: they taste good when cooked.

The trouble with this tree, however, is that it's a tropical all the way. It quits growing when the weather gets cool, and freezes to the ground during a frost. Fortunately, Moringa is hard to kill and, in spring, will generally come back from its roots. Crop them low, and treat them like a vegetable.

Plant moringa seeds or stick cuttings in the desired locations. Watch them shoot to the moon, and harvest leaves as desired. Cut back the trees to 3–4 feet, and harvest lots of new growth to dry for storage. Put a 2-foot diameter ring of chicken wire around the base of the tree, and fill with straw of fall leaves to protect against frost. Cut off all top growth and save the leaves to eat, then cover the cut trunk. If you have wet winters, I also recommend putting a tarp over the wire and leaves to keep the trunk from rotting. Wait until after all danger of frost the next year, and then remove the ring and straw. *Boom!* Moringa flies back into action as soon as days warm, and you'll be harvesting fresh leaves again.

The trees I protected from frost came back with significantly more vigor than those I simply let freeze to the ground, though I've never had them make pods in my colder location. This may be due to the high soil nutrition and plenty of water in my gardens, as friends nearby had theirs make pods. Setting fruit seems to be related to a combination of stresses, including dry ground and poor soil. In the Caribbean they lost their leaves and were covered with pods at the height of the dry season.

Mustard

Mustard greens are easy to grow and remarkably healthy for you; allegedly, they even fight off cancer cells. Though it's not as cold-hardy as kale or collards, mustard takes quite a bit of frost before dying. Mine have survived the mid-20s without damage. In fact, if you want success, you cannot plant these during the warm part of the year. If you do, the plants rapidly bolt and peter out. Plant in early spring or after the heat of summer for a fall crop.

Boiled mustard has a texture and flavor we prefer to its cousin collards. Stir-fried, it has a spicy bitterness the kids don't really like, and I agree with the kids. Serve cut mustard with other leaves. Rather like its cousin horseradish, it's a bit rough to eat alone.

Mustard germinates quickly and you can start harvesting leaves in about a month. Depending on the variety, you can get purple leaves... curly leaves... or even huge leaves. I cut off leaves as I want them, and the plant continually produces new ones. Twenty-four plants was more than enough for my large family.

When it gets warm and mustard goes to seed, you can easily save the seeds (they dry inside the seed pods and will shatter and fall everywhere, so don't wait too long to harvest!) and grind them with vinegar to make table mustard.

If you haven't done it before, set aside some space for mustard this year—it's well-worth growing.

Okra

What? You want to actually eat okra? I'll bet you've got a great recipe for Okra Eggplant Stew, don't you?

Well, if you insist, I'll tell you how to grow it.

Plant okra in spring or summer after all danger of frost and when the soil is nice and warm. It grows quickly and will bear pods in about two months. Keep them picked. They grow rapidly and get tough when too large.

Don't plant okra in the same place more than once every couple of years since the nematodes love okra, and their populations will build up in the soil. Alternating with mustard is a good idea.

Once you've harvested your okra, I recommend you throw the pods away, then put the plants on the compost pile.

I'm kidding. I used to really dislike okra but over the years I've come to love it. It thrives in the heat and produces abundantly and if well-grown, has a very pleasant flavor as well as beautiful flowers. If you can get past the slimy texture, it's good stuff.

Onions

Onions can be grown from "sets" or seeds. Sets are just little onions sold in bags that you can plant and let grow into big onions in your garden.

Some onions are easier to grow than others. There are a lot of options, including Egyptian "walking onions," the rare I'itoi onions, green bunching onions, red onions, sweet onions, potato onions...

It's a big family. Most are pretty easy to grow. Plant in the spring in a really cold climate or give them a go in the fall in a warmer climate. Some, like the walking onions, make good perennials and will produce for years if they're happy.

The greens of onions are edible and make a good condiment similar to chives. My wife plants store-bought onions that have sprouted green tops, lets them grow bigger, then harvests leaves with scissors for soups.

Peas

Before I get into this plant, let me get one thing straight: in a survival situation—or even a pinched grocery budget—peas wouldn't be my first choice as a staple. They're a lot of work for only a little food. Fortunately for them, they aren't useful for their peas alone.

The common garden pea is not just a tasty cool-season vegetable, it's also a nitrogen fixer and a decent producer of fast-decomposing organic matter. If you grow various field pea varieties, you can get a decent yield of dry peas without too much work. It's certainly less work than shelling green peas.

When I put new ground into circulation, I have some cold-weather green manures I like to throw down before planting serious crops. Peas, along with lentils and chick peas, and occasionally rye grass or turnips, are some of my favorites. If you're lucky, you can get bags of whole dried peas in the grocery store. They're also often available in big bags at farm-oriented retailers. I use peas more for ground-covering nitrogen fixers than anything else. Anytime there's a gap in my fall, spring and winter gardens, I try to tuck in some peas. If they produce peas for me—great. If they don't, they're still feeding the soil and making biomass for my compost.

I've been known to chop them down in spring and plant peppers and other transplants right into their newly mulched remains.

Another thing about peas that many don't know: you can eat the leaves and shoots in salads. They're a pleasant, crunchy, vaguely pea-flavored green that mixes well with other common salad ingredients. And of course, the young pods can be stir-fried (note that they're stringy unless you get an edible-podded snow-pea type variety).

All that said—go ahead. Plant some peas as the world burns. Just don't expect to get fat off them.

Peppers

I once told a friend with a T-shirt company that he should print shirts reading:

Make Mine Thai Hot

Because Nothing Says "Yummy" Like Rectal Bleeding!

For some reason, he refused.

I've grown Thai peppers, bell peppers, habaneros, purple-black spicy peppers, jalapeños, scotch bonnets, Tabasco peppers, bird peppers, Grenadian seasoning peppers and lots of brilliant red cayennes.

Hot peppers are easy to grow if you have a warm summer and somewhat fertile soil. Bell peppers also like warm conditions but they also like good soil and regular water. They also suffer more from pests and rot issues than the hot pepper varieties I've grown. If you give them plenty of sunshine and lots of compost, they should do well. And if they don't, at least you'll have your Thai peppers.

Peppers will usually keep producing in the heat and even through the summer when tomatoes and almost everything else gives up.

I have discovered that the one pepper that really manages to produce excellently and tastes great with no care is the regular old cayenne pepper. Despite my poor planning, I've managed to grow them for years without much preparation or thought—and I'm always glad to have their delicious smoky kick in my wife's stir-fried meals.

Most hot peppers are perennial in non-freezing climates. I've seen a 6-foot tall pepper plant down in South Florida that was multiple years old. That said, if you get a nasty frost, they'll die.

To grow peppers, plant the seeds in flats or in the ground after the last frost date. They grow quickly and bear in about three months. Interestingly, I've also had them self-seed here and there around my gardens. Occasionally, I'd toss a rotten pepper aside, or throw some in the compost... and a little baby would come up. If I liked its location, I'd leave it. If not, I'd transplant it into a bed. My bet is that cayennes in particular are pretty close to being a wild pepper. They're tough, and they're attractive plants to boot.

The only pest problems I've had with these guys involve stink bugs. They'll ruin a few peppers here and there by punching their nasty mouth parts into them and leaving spots that rot—yet even with those losses, we end up with plenty of peppers.

For making salsa, jalapeños excel in juiciness and good raw flavor; in brutal heat and smokiness, habaneros are king. For a mild pepper for packing with cheese and rice, poblanos are tops.

My favorite use for hot peppers, and particularly cayennes, is as ground red pepper. I picked up a Braun coffee grinder at the thrift store for $1.75 and use that for turning dried peppers into powder. I've also smoked hot peppers and mixed them with a little sugar, salt, and vinegar to make incredible hot sauces.

As a survival plant, peppers aren't the best since you can't live on them, but they sure do add flavor to the things you can eat. There are also proven benefits to consuming hot peppers, such as improved circulation and Looking Cool When Around Your Peers.

Potatoes

Potatoes are probably the ultimate survival crop: they tolerate poor soil, bear abundantly, handle a variety of climates, and are packed with calories. Space-wise, they beat the living daylights out of grains, plus they store for a long period. In some climates, you can plant potatoes in spring and fall and get a double harvest. If you pick purple varieties, they are high in healthful anthocyanins, although the yields I have had from them are much lower than their white or red cousins.

The best yielding potatoes I've planted are russets, but your mileage may vary. Russet types also seem to store much better than thinner-skinned red and yellow varieties. That said, Yukon gold potatoes have a very nice flavor when baked, and red types are great in potato salad. If you have a hotter summer, russets don't do as well, however. Kennebec potatoes are a good alternative for the south.

Growing potatoes is easy: in early spring, a few weeks before your last expected frost date, dig narrow trenches that are about half a foot deep, and drop in chopped potatoes with good eyes on each piece. If you are scared of knives, you can use whole potatoes. I like to space them about a foot apart down the trench. Cover the potatoes with loose soil and wait.

A few weeks later, they will start coming up. The plants will grow about 2 feet tall, will usually bloom, turn yellow, and die after a few months. Once the above ground growth dies, start digging.

NOTE: When you dig potatoes, don't leave the roots lying around in the sun for any period of time, since the sunlight encourages the tubers to produce a toxin called solanine. This makes you feel lousy, particularly in your back and joints. Better to avoid it by bringing your potatoes in quickly, and letting them dry out in the shade, then storing them in a cool, dark place. Covered baskets, or brown paper bags work well. If you are interested in saving potatoes to plant the next year, only save healthy-looking potatoes from healthy-looking plants.

Although potatoes are a perennial plant, they suffer from a wide range of diseases; most of these problems can be solved via proper crop rotation. Don't plant them on the same ground in subsequent years, or you'll be totally asking for trouble.

One more thing on potatoes: they can be grown from seed if you are a plant geek with time on your hands. They'll produce little green tomato-like fruit, filled with tiny seeds. If you plant those seeds, they'll grow into little potato plants, which will grow in size, then die back. When they die back, dig them up, and take some of the tiny tubers that result; when you plant those the next season, you'll be able to grow them into full-size plants that bear full-size roots.

If you taste any of these potatoes and find them bitter, chuck them. The bitterness means that the seed has reverted to a toxic precursor of modern cultivated potatoes. That aside, if I wanted to grow lots of food fast in a crash, potatoes would be at the top of the list, particularly if I lived in a cooler climate. Learn to grow these, and you'll be eating French fries through the apocalypse.

As a final note, if the government takes away all our guns, don't forget: potato guns are easy to construct from a piece of PVC with a firing chamber and an ignition.

Grow your own ammunition!

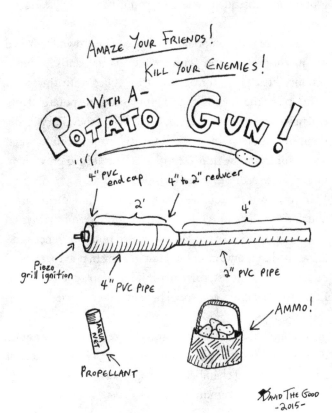

Radishes

Radishes are super-easy to grow. When I was a kid they were one of my first crops since I read the back of all the seed packages and said that radishes were ready to harvest faster than anything else. Sometimes you can get ready-to-eat radishes at just 28 days after germination!

Radishes are a cool-season crop and will go right to seed without setting good roots if you plant them too late in the spring. I plant them a few weeks before the last expected frost date, and the little frosts don't hurt them. I also plant them in the fall.

One of my favorite radishes is the big Japanese Daikon. They are huge and, as long as the weather is cool, they also have a mild sweet flavor.

Spinach

Grow spinach the same way you grow lettuce. See above.

Squash and Pumpkins

Winter squash is a great survival crop.

If I were to rank crops according to ease of growing, productivity, storability, and nutrition, winter squash and pumpkins would be in my top five.

Winter squashes include lots of old heirloom varieties such as Boston Marrow, Hubbard, Cheese pumpkins and more well-known types such as butternut, spaghetti, acorn, and delicatas.

Hot climate varieties include large long-necked calabazas from central America and the ancient Florida heirloom Seminole pumpkin.

Halloween pumpkins and the giant types exhibited at fairs are some of the least tasty squashes, so don't judge the whole family on those.

Plant winter squash in compost-amended hills or melon pits after all danger of frost. They love to grow on compost. Some of my best harvests have been from accidental seedlings popping up in the compost and giving me tons of squash.

When the rinds of squash are hard to dent with your fingernail, they're mature. I also look at the stems at the top of the fruit. If they're yellow rather than green, it's time to harvest. I cut the stem with a pair of pruning shears and leave at least an inch of stem on the top of the squash. This helps them keep longer. Some types, like Seminole pumpkins, can keep for over a year just sitting on a shelf at room temperature. Others will go bad in just a few months.

Winter squashes taste best if you let them sit for at least a few weeks after harvest. The flavor sweetens and becomes richer over this time, and it's worth the wait.

Unlike winter squashes, summer squash are harvested as a vegetable before mature. They're good for the table, grilling, and salads, but they're not a survival staple like a mature winter squash.

When you find a variety of squash you like, let the fruits mature completely and save the seeds. If you're growing more than one type on your homestead, however, be aware that many squashes will cross with each other and give you strange combinations. This can be good or bad. If you're lucky, you'll end up with a totally new breed you can name after yourself. If you're unlucky, you might get bad-keeping bland squash that looks like a shrunken head. Chances are, however, that whatever you get will be great.

Sugarcane

You can grow sugarcane successfully all the way up into Georgia and probably beyond, even without having a marsh. It grows fine on drier land, so long as it gets some water. Since it's a perennial plant, once you plant sugarcane you can look forward to having it for years.

The hardest part about growing sugarcane might be finding the plants in the first place. I've never seen it for sale at a plant nursery. Ask for sugarcane and you're likely to get a blank look and the question, "does that even grow here?"

All you need is a good hunk of sugarcane with a couple of intact nodes (those are the joints in the cane). Since sugarcane is usually harvested in the fall, that's the time you're likely to see the canes for sale. Most grocery stores don't carry sugarcane, but some farm stands and ethnic markets do in the fall—and fall is when you want to plant.

When you get home from buying sugarcane, cut your canes into segments with at least 3–4 nodes each, pick a good spot to plant them, then put those pieces on their sides about 4–6 inches down, and cover them up. All winter, those pieces will sit down there in the ground until the soil warms up in the spring. When I plant sugarcane in November, the plants always pop up for me sometime in March or April. For each cane you bury, you'll usually get a couple of good shoots emerging from the ground.

If you really don't want to trust the earth to take care of your little baby sugarcane plants, you can just stick some chunks of cane in pots with a node or two beneath the dirt and keep them someplace that doesn't freeze, like a sunroom. They'll grow.

When my baby sugarcane plants appear in the spring—and I'm pretty sure it's not going to freeze again—I fertilize them with chicken manure. You can also use lawn fertilizer since they're a grass and they like lots of nitrogen. Throughout the summer they'll get nice and tall, and sometime in July or August you'll really see the canes starting to thicken up, but don't chop them yet unless you really can't stand to wait. Wait until it's just about time for the first frost of fall, then go cut the canes down—that way you'll get the largest harvest possible.

If you don't cut them down and you get a freeze, you're going to lose all the aboveground growth and you may even lose the plants. Harvest by cutting the canes down close to the ground, and then put the sugarcane roots to bed for the winter by mulching over them with some rough material. Leaves are good for this, but any mulch works. My sugarcane came back even when I barely mulched over the roots. In its second year, sugarcane will bunch out and hopefully give you a few more canes than it did the first year, which means you'll be able to share the abundance.

Pressing out the sugar is difficult and requires good equipment or some redneck ingenuity. I figured out how to make cane syrup without a press. You can find photos and details on my website: www.thesurvivalgardener.com/how-to-make-cane-syrup-at-home-without-a-press/.

Sugar cane may not be a top priority survival crop, but having a source of sugar would surely be nice in a crash.

Sweet Potatoes

Sweet potatoes are misunderstood. They're confused with yams, lumped in with white potatoes in many growing guides, and rarely utilized to their fullest potential.

These babies are energy-rich, nutritionally dense, and potential lifesavers in a major downturn. If you're not growing them, it's time to put them in your plans.

If you live in USDA growing zone 9 or 10, sweet potatoes are very impressive perennials. Further north, frosts prevent them from living up to their complete potential, but even as an annual they give a lot of bang for their buck.

The first thing needed for growing sweet potatoes is prop-agative material, i.e., roots or slips. You've probably stuck toothpicks in a sweet potato, half-submerged the potato in a glass of water, then watched vines grow out of the top. As a kid, I did this multiple times and always enjoyed watching the ivy-like vines emerge and tumble across the counter. Of course, eventually the root in the water would rot and make an amazing smell, which would then motivate Mom to banish the offending tuber from the house.

What I didn't know back then was this: when vines emerge from the top of the sweet potato, you can break them off when they're a few inches long and new ones will grow. Plant the little vines, and you're well on your way to growing lots more potatoes. This can be done multiple times off one toothpick-impaled root. I find that just laying roots on their sides in a flat of potting soil and letting them send up vines over and over again works even better and never ends up rotting like the ones in water.

I start all my sweet potato beds each year from a handful of little leftover roots from the previous year's harvest. We start slips in the greenhouse and on windowsills in January and February and plant at the end of March, through April and even into May. Your local dates may vary, but having a few months to start propagating before planting is a big help. Don't plant until all danger of frost has passed.

Of course, if it's spring and you've already got a plant or two in the ground and want to start more, you can simply chop off chunks of the vine and plant them here and there. Just stick

1-foot pieces into the ground, right-side up. Water them, and they'll root.

Sweet potatoes have a vining habit and will often produce roots where the vines touch the ground, though the majority of the potatoes are located at the base of each plant. Last year we planted about 30 slips and harvested about 120 pounds of roots. This was a nice yield, especially considering I barely did anything more than plant, wait, and harvest.

One thing to consider when you plant sweet potatoes: they spread like crazy. I planted them in my wife's rose garden one year, and they basically crushed the roses. On the upside, I got a crate of potatoes. On the downside, my wife cried for three weeks over her silly flowers. I explained to her that you can't really eat roses during TEOTWAWKI, but it didn't help.

If you want to get a really good yield on your sweet potatoes, get them in the ground as early as possible. This is a double-edged sword, though, since sweet potatoes are not cold-hardy. You need a long season to grow them, but if they freeze, they're dead. So— early as possible means early as possible *after* the danger of frost.

Sweet potatoes like lots of compost and thrive in mulched beds. Don't overfeed them, however, since that will lead to an abundance of vines with small roots. I spray them occasionally with a weak foliar fertilizer, and they do great. I also till in bone meal, cottonseed meal, compost, 10-10-10, or whatever I have laying around.

Since I grow sweet potatoes organically, I do have some trouble with bugs chewing the leaves and occasionally boring their way through the roots. The losses are minimal, however. Sweet potatoes are tough. Just don't keep growing them in the same place, or you may end up with pest issues.

When it starts getting cold outside, it's time to harvest what you have. If you wait too long, frosts can burn the plants and rot your potatoes. When you harvest them, be gentle. You want the skins to stay as intact as possible to keep them from rotting in storage.

I harvest sweet potatoes during a dry day in autumn, then spread them out on my back porch in the shade. They stay there for a week or two to dry and cure. I turn them occasionally to make sure they dry out evenly, then gather the most intact spuds and store them in cardboard boxes or wicker baskets in the dark. The uglier and damaged spuds get eaten first, and the little ones are set aside for the next year's seed.

My children eat a lot of sweet potatoes during fall and winter. They store for months in our pantry and taste better when they've sat for a couple of weeks out of the ground. Our favorite way to enjoy them is baked with lots of butter. They're good for breakfast, lunch, and dinner.

Note: if you have longer winters, you may want to can sweet potatoes. I know a local prepper who cans vast quantities of them every fall. In my opinion, they pale beside fresh roots—but still, it's better than starving.

Beyond the roots themselves, the extensive vines make a great mulch/compost at the end of the year. I throw piles of them into my food forest around the base of needy trees and let them rot down.

Roots—damaged, bug-eaten, or tiny—make good chicken feed. My birds seem to prefer them cooked, but they'll still peck away at chopped raw ones when they feel like it.

In warm climates, sweet potatoes make an excellent, dense ground cover for food forests (if you live in a tropical or subtropical area, you might enjoy my inspiring little book *Create Your Own Florida Food Forest*). I've planted them here, and they've come back year after year, although I don't get many roots, thanks to the shade.

One final note on sweet potatoes: although the roots are excellent, the greens are a good vegetable in their own right. We eat them raw in salads, sauté them in stir-fries, and cook them as greens. In salads they're a somewhat bland filler, but cooked ones have a nice texture. If you did this with white potato greens, you'd start aching and throwing up from solanine poisoning. Try it with true yams, and you'll likely sterilize yourself.

Sweet potatoes stand out from the crowd! They won't cause vomiting or sterility!

Now if I could just cross them with roses, all would be right with the world.

Tobacco

If the world falls apart, you're going to want tobacco. Even if you're a non-smoker, the barter value of this sacred Native American plant is very high—and the number of individuals growing it is very low. Therefore, economics dictates that the gardener who is growing tobacco after tobacco disappears from shelves is going to be a very rich man.

Tobacco is easy to grow once established in the garden; however, getting it started is a bit tricky. The reason for this is twofold: first of all, the seeds are very tiny; second of all, they require light and moisture to germinate.

What this means in practice is that you have to sprinkle the seeds on top of the soil and keep them well-lit and moist at the same time. Since the seeds are so tiny, they dry out quickly in the sun, and new shoots will wither away and disappear on a hot day if you aren't watching out for them.

There are a few ways you can get around this. I simply fill a flat with fine posting soil mixed with compost. The flats don't have to be anything special. I make them out of scrap wood. All it takes is a square or rectangular frame of wood with more slats of wood nailed on the bottom to hold in the dirt. Three to four inches deep is good enough. You can also use plastic trays or whatever holds soil—just make sure it drains well. Soppy soil often kills little plants.

Once I have my planting flat, I place it in indirect sunlight (my back porch is perfect) and then sprinkle tobacco seeds generously across the surface of the soil. I then mist it well with a spray bottle of water. Then, every day, multiple times a day, I mist the surface again as I think about it. This goes on for usually 10–14 days until I see lots of little shoots popping up... and then I keep misting those. Tobacco sprouts are really, really tiny—a gardener almost needs to get out his magnifying glass to see them when they first emerge from the soil.

Another method for germinating tobacco seeds is to simply mist the flat well and then cover it with plastic wrap to keep in the moisture and cut down on your need to water.

This spring I started tobacco seeds in a flat of moisture-control potting soil which stays wetter than regular potting soil and they have done great without the bother of misting or covering. This is my new favorite method.

Once your baby tobacco plants are up and growing, it's time to thin. I use a pair of fine scissors (hair-cutting scissors are good) to snip out about half of the shoots or more, giving each little tobacco plant at least an inch of space around its base to grow. As they get to around 1-inch tall, I thin again or transplant them to another new flat at 4-inch spacing. A spoon makes a good trowel. As the plants grow, I try to make sure they get more direct sunlight during the day so they can adapt before making their way into my garden.

When your tobacco plants reach about 4–6 inches in height, they're ready to be planted in their final location.

Give them decent soil and nitrogen, and they'll grow very rapidly. I harvest leaves as they get big and put them inside to dry. I've also dried them all over the dashboard of my car by cracking open the windows and parking the vehicle in the sun. This works very quickly and gives your car a nice sweet tobacco aroma. It makes for a harsh smoke, however.

Curing tobacco isn't necessary in order to smoke it but it does give the final product a better flavor. Methods for this abound, yet I've found just stringing the leaves on thread and hanging them in my barn for a year makes them taste pretty good. For a Latakia-style English pipe tobacco, soak them in water and molasses, then stuff the sopping wet and sticky leaves into your smoker for a few hours with the wood chips of your choice. This makes for a hearty, leathery, smoky tobacco that's great to puff while you ponder the fate of man.

Some tobacco growers top their plants before they bloom to increase leaf size, though I haven't done this. Usually, since I harvest as I go, I get plenty of good leaves and still am able to save seeds from the plants by letting them bloom and go to seed in the garden. Hummingbirds like the tubular flowers and seem to visit regularly. Maybe it's like a smoke break for them. They'll hit the blooms, go off, do something else, come back... have some more. I wonder if they start biting their nails or buying gum when the tobacco season comes to a close...

Saving seed is easy: just let the tobacco pods dry on the plant and then bring them inside to dry completely. Each pod has thousands of tiny seeds inside—enough for acres of marvelous nicotine.

Tomatoes

I hate growing tomatoes, but that's mostly because I live in one of the hardest places to grow them. The problem is, they're pretty much the most popular plant gardeners want to grow, so if I don't write about them you'll get mad and give me a one-star review on Amazon.

So, here goes.

Tomatoes are called a vegetable, but they're actually a fruit. This is really profound and will get you extra sexy points when you casually mention it to young women in the grocery store. Someone once said, "knowledge is knowing a tomato is a fruit—wisdom is knowing it doesn't belong in a fruit salad."

So far I've filled in two paragraphs and told you nothing about how to grow tomatoes.

All right, I'll work for those five stars.

Tomatoes are a warm-season crop that absolutely thrives on compost. I find the easiest types to grow are the cherry types, followed by Roma or "paste" types, then other mid-sized tomatoes, and then, at the toughest end of the spectrum, beefsteaks. In the tropics, we ran a tomato trial and had the best luck with an heirloom variety named "Carbon," which is a nice slicing variety.

In my opinion, the paste types are the best for a survival garden because they're the best for preserving as tomato sauce, stewed tomatoes, etc. They contain more flesh and less water which makes them a lot quicker to process than their juicier friends. I have made canned tomato sauce from juicy eating types, and it takes a long time to cook them down to a good consistency for canning.

Like their cousins eggplant, tobacco, and peppers, tomatoes can't take the cold. Plant transplants or direct seed in good soil—preferably with lots of compost in it—after the last frost date. Tomatoes usually start coming in about three months later, depending on variety, and are then usually destroyed by insects as they ripen. Everything in the world wants to eat tomatoes.

Then there's the rot... the splitting fruit when it's been dry and then rains for a week... the trellises that collapse... the blossom end rot... the... the... the.... (sobs)

I thought I was going to get through this bit on... to... toma... tomatoes without breaking down. I can't even say it without pain. I really did think I could do it, but it's too painful. Please don't give me one star. You don't know how traumatic these cruel red fruits are for me. I have Post Tomato Stress Disorder. Please have pity.

Okay - enough joking for now. If you don't live in the humid south, tomatoes aren't nearly as hard to grow. In Middle Tennessee we did great with a wide variety of types. They like good soil, good support, regular irrigation and sharp eyes so you can catch the hornworms before they eat entire plants. If you want a huge amount of expert advice on tomato growing, check out the film "Tomatoes: From Seed to Sauce" on YouTube, where I interview three top experts on the how to grow tomatoes.

Tree Collards

Tree collards are a great perennial vegetable related to cabbage, kale, and yes, collards. They grow from cuttings rather than seeds, and if your climate is mild enough, they can live for years.

This means you need to pick a good permanent spot for your tree collard patch: after receiving severe coffee burns in a strange "accident," I no longer recommend growing them in your wife's rose garden.

During the winter tree collards are sweeter in flavor than they are in the summer. Chickens love them, and collards are quite nutritious, so plant extra for the poultry, and toss collards in whenever you think about it. Tree collards are so easy to start from cuttings, it just makes sense.

Turnips

Turnips have fallen out of favor over the years. They used to be a very popular vegetable but tastes have changed.

They should change back! First of all, turnips are very good for you, and second of all, they're also very easy to grow. They can be used to fatten hogs, they grow in colder climates, they keep the ground covered, and they look pretty. Additionally, they store well, can be harvested over a decent length of season, and the greens are a good vegetable all on their own. I think the greens often taste better than the roots. Some turnip varieties are grown solely for their leaves. If you like roots, make sure you didn't buy seed for those cultivars. The roots of the "leaf" varieties of turnips are woody and worthless.

In the past I grew a lot of purple-top turnips but I have discovered "White Egg" and "White Lady" turnips taste a whole lot better. They're even sweet enough to eat raw in slices, whereas the purple top types just aren't great no matter how you slice them.

I plant my turnips in the fall via broadcasting them over disturbed soil. I then rake and water them in. If you're planting a small space, just plant the seeds at a nice spacing. I prefer chucking them, of course, but you may have other, more neurotic preferences. They come up in a week or so and grow rapidly. I tend to be able to pull my first turnips in perhaps two months or so. The harvest doesn't usually happen all at once. I usually get a few early monsters, followed by a stream of turnips hitting harvest size for weeks and weeks after that. Turnips do not like the heat, so don't plant them too late.

If you live in a colder climate, plant turnips in the summer for a fall harvest, or in the early spring. If things get tough, you're going to want these guys. They'll keep you alive, are undemanding, and have very few problems.

Yams

Across much of the Deep South, there's a vigorous and attractive climbing vine called the "air potato." Its Latin name is *Dioscorea bulbifera*. This basically pest-free plant (with the exception of this crazy red beetle the University of Florida has purposely released to attack it) has the strange habit of forming dangling bulbils (aerial roots) along its vines. When fall comes and the day lengths shorten, the vines dry up and the bulbils, which look sort of like little potatoes, fall to the ground for the winter. In spring, each one grows into a new plant. By this manner, air potato plants spread happily over acres of woods and have become the bane of native plant enthusiasts, forestry departments, and homeowners. You see, the air potato isn't originally from the US. It's from Africa and Asia. And though some forms are edible and are a great staple, other forms are inedible since they contain a toxic steroid that can mess with your reproductive system and make you vomit. Though I've done hours of research on *D. bulbifera*, I still haven't come across a way to know which wild types are edible and which aren't. This is unfortunate, since it's very prolific. If you can manage to get ahold of a known edible type, they're worth growing. Just imagine potatoes hanging on a vine!

To make things more confusing, *Dioscorea bulbifera* has a cousin, *Dioscorea alata*, also sometimes called an "air potato," which is always edible and is a very good crop for survivalists in the right climate. The reason I started with *D. bulbifera* is to make sure you don't randomly start digging roots in the wild and eating them. Unless you like sterility and vomiting, stay away from air potatoes unless you know for sure they're an edible type.

Unlike *D. bulbifera*, *D. alata*, the "winged yam" (also known as ube, purple yam, and roughly one billion other regional names) has dark and misshapen bulbils that look like grotesque charred animal organs. The "air potatoes" on *D. bulbifera* are pocked, light tan to dark brown, and much rounder, with a look that's reminiscent of little moons or asteroids.

Like its cousin *D. bulbifera*, the winged yam is also classified as an invasive species in some states. Though it's not nearly as aggressive, someone decided to add it to the list years ago. This makes it hard to find for sale, though wild specimens can be obtained on occasion.

Do you ever feel like there's a conspiracy against us when it comes to growing staple foods and useful plants? Along with opium poppies (which can be used safely to treat diarrhea, headaches, and toothaches), mesquite trees (which have excellent wood, nitrogen-fixing ability, and edible pods), hemp (which has amazing medicinal, fiber, and biomass uses) and water spinach (which will produce lots of nutritious leaves in a tiny space), you can stick the winged yam on the list of exceptional species which are just not appreciated by The Powers That Be.

Look, you almost certainly won't get in trouble for growing this thing, but you're not allowed to sell or spread it around. Unlike, say, *Cannabis sativa*, it's basically unrecognizable except to plant geeks, and it doesn't really go as well with Cheetos and scratchy old Bob Marley records. Plus, it's just a somewhat invasive plant, not a drug. Nobody is going to form cartels, write rap songs, or become prostitutes over winged yams. Seriously. (Except for the rap songs. I wrote a few yam-related rap songs.)

The winged yam is a perennial species of true yam (not to be confused with sweet potatoes) that grows huge, delicious roots with very little care from the gardener. Basically, you plant a bulbil in the fall, winter, or spring, then wait. In late spring, when the yam has decided it's warm enough, a little vine will pop out of the ground and start looking for something to climb. That vine will grow rapidly and reach for the sky, whether in shade or sun. As the year progresses, the plant gathers plenty of energy from sunlight and stores it in a rapidly expanding tuber beneath the earth. As fall arrives, bulbils form at various leaf nodes and dangle in the air as the vine yellows and dies back. At this point, the root can be dug, or it can be left in the ground for another year to continue growing in size.

Why would you want to grow these puppies? How about this: the roots can hit 80 pounds or more. Not only that, they're delicious. I know a lot of people brag about the flavor of various wild stuff they've tried, but in the case of this yam, it's not hyperbole. The tubers taste as good or better than potatoes. As an aside, some cultivars are purple, though the white varieties are much more common in the States.

Beyond the size and flavor, this is a "set and forget" crop. If you plant these in your garden, all you have to do is wait. It will grow in bad soil, beneath trees, in abandoned lots, along fences, without watering, etc. This is probably where some of its "invasive" reputation comes in. It lives, and it makes plenty of food without any work on your part. It's also unrecognizable as food to most people. Yet overseas, this plant is literally a lifesaver in some communities. Yes, *D. alata* can invade native ecosystems; however, what if we simply ate it instead of calling in guys with backpack sprayers full of RoundUp™? I've done my fair share in harvesting them from the woods, and if you keep an eye on the plants you grow, you'll easily be able to keep them from escaping. And even if they do escape—it's not like the state is ever going to win this fight. *D. alata* has been kicking around here and there for almost a century. Having edible yams in the woods simply means there will be more wild food available during times of crisis or famine.

Giant roots, little care, easy growing and great taste make the winged yam a perfect prepper plant—even if it's not appreciated by your local agricultural extension.

Beyond *D. alata*, there are other yams you can find and grow, including *D. cayenensis* (the yellow yam), *D. rotundata* (the white yam), *D. opposita* (the Chinese yam, which has small edible aerial bulbils. Eric Toensmeier calls them "yamberries" in his entertaining book *Paradise Lot*) and lots more. *D. opposita* is quite cold hardy, unlike most yams, so if you live north of USDA Zone 8, I recommend giving that one a try.

Yaupon Holly

This is a plant I'd wager few survivalists are growing, and that's a shame.

If you've ever had yerba mate tea, it's made from a tropical cousin of the yaupon holly and has a very similar earthy flavor, plus plenty of caffeine.

Yaupon holly, however, has an unfortunate Latin name. It's *Ilex vomitoria*. Apparently, yaupon got this name thanks to an early encounter the Spanish had with it. The story goes that a group of Native Americans invited the Spanish to a party in which they made gallons of strong black tea from the Yaupon holly, then drank prodigious quantities of the caffeine-rich stuff and started going nuts, dancing, and then vomiting. The Spanish decided that the holly tea probably wasn't for them and passed along the tale of this "vomiting holly," which gave it an unfair Latin name and wrecked what could have been a great new tea industry for the New World.

Why do I say the Latin name is unfair? Because the tea doesn't contain any purgatives. Yaupon holly brews into a nice, pleasant, smoky tea that's quite comparable to a decent green tea or light yerba mate flavor. If you drink a gallon of it—or just about anything—you may throw up, but this is to be expected and is no fault of this noble little tree.

Yaupon holly can be grown through most of the Confederacy and probably somewhat beyond that range. I've brewed it into a tea by boiling the green leaves fresh or dried. I've also tossed them on a cast-iron pan until browned and then brewed it. This give a little richer smoky flavor and is alleged to release more of the plant's caffeine.

Yaupon hollies are often sold as a native landscape tree or shrub. There are columnar cultivars, dwarf types and larger spreading types. They're beautiful small to mid-sized trees that fit well into the landscaping and into a hidden source of caffeine.

Look, you don't want to fight zombies without caffeine, do you? I wouldn't. Plant a yaupon, and you'll be able to easily grow what you need for a morning cup of pick-me-up.

Zucchini

Zucchini is nasty. I'm not telling you how to grow it. I simply refuse.

Chapter 8

Preserving the Harvest

Once you've brought in your crops, preservation is key to ensuring you'll have enough to eat during the winter and through droughts and bad years.

Some crops, such as grains, are very easy to preserve. You simply let them dry out, then pack them away in sacks or buckets. If insects are a problem, you can add some diatomaceous earth to your grain, or, if you have access to dry ice, you can put some in the top of the buckets when you pack them so the container fills with carbon dioxide and renders it impossible for grain-destroying pests to breathe.

A few of the crops in chapter seven can be grown right through a mild winter, yet unless you live in the tropics where it never freezes or have abundant game and know how to hunt it, chances are the winter will be a hungry season on the homestead. One cannot live on kale alone.

Quite a few crops, such as cabbages, storage apples, winter squash, and most roots, can be kept for a long time in a homemade root cellar or cool basement so long as it doesn't freeze. Beyond these simple methods, let's look at the four major long-term storage methods you'll want to learn in case of a collapse.

Canning

Canning has gained new popularity in recent years. I know lots of people who can everything from jam to potatoes and beef stew to salsa. Mason jars are a hot commodity in prepper circles, and their ease of use makes them a worthwhile addition to your survival stockpile.

For those unfamiliar with the dynamics of canning, Mason jars are jars with standardized lid sizes (there's a common size and a wide-mouth variant). The lid is made up of two parts: a ring and a lid with a rubber gasket under its lip. When the jar is filled almost to the top with liquid, capped and screwed shut, then heated, some of the air inside is forced out. Later, as the contents of the jar cools, a vacuum is created inside which pulls the gasket tight and indents the top of the lid, giving you visual confirmation that the jar is safely sealed.

Foods can be canned in a boiling water bath (I use a big stockpot) or in a pressure canner. Though the water bath method is easier and cheaper, it's not suitable for many foods.

Here's the tougher part: canning requires that you know which foods are safe to water bath can and which foods require pressure canning. Why does this matter? Because if you get it wrong, you can end up dead or paralyzed. Botulism is an illness that becomes a risk when you have anaerobic solutions of food without enough acid or salt to keep *Clostridium botulinum* spores from developing into toxin-producing bacteria. The spores are destroyed when food is heated to 250 degrees, which only happens in a pressure cooker, not in a standard water bath.

Now that I've scared you, take a deep breath. People have been canning for a long, long time, and the modern methods are very safe. If you want to get serious about home canning, buy *The Ball Complete Book of Home Preserving*. It's the best guide on the topic and will ensure your complete safety. If you like to see how canning happens rather than just read about it, another good resource is the two-hour instructional film created by my friend Kendra Lynne titled *At Home Canning for Beginners and Beyond*. That will give you a good start.

The rules of thumb are pretty simple. Low-acid foods, such as green beans, chicken breast, potatoes, and most vegetables, need to be canned in a pressure canner at higher temperatures, whereas high-sugar and acidic foods, such as jams, vinegar-based hot sauces, and pickles, can be canned safely in a water bath canner.

A little known fact is that salsa jars and other glass containers with rubber rims under their lids and pop-up style buttons can be re-used as canning containers. If the button pops up while they're stored in the pantry, however, throw them out. That goes for your Mason jars as well. The button is there to show you that the food is still safely sterile and vacuum-packed. Don't trust anything that's popped!

Though my favorite method is to grow as much food as possible year-round and eat fresh from the garden, canning allows the prepper to store in the fat times and preserve a large bounty for the lean times.

When I lived in Tennessee my pear trees would overflow with pears in the fall. We'd process them into pear butter, pear salsa, pear sauce, and sliced pears in syrup. It was great! We were able to enjoy those pears year-round on the years where we really got our act together and spent a couple of days packing jars and storing the harvest.

If you have a long winter, canning is vital to holding on to more of what you grow. Instead of just giving away all the extra—or worse, letting it rot—can when there's an abundance so you can eat when fresh produce is thin. Just do it right!

Drying

Drying is a tried and true method of preservation dating back to the beginning of time. By removing the moisture from fruits and vegetables, decay is halted, and microorganisms are unable to take hold and convert them into stinking slime.

If you've had banana chips, raisins, or dried apple slices, you know how delicious dried foods can be. I've dehydrated strawberries, mushrooms, okra (amazingly, it still kept its disgusting mucilaginous texture when re-hydrated!), pears, peppers, pumpkin, moringa, and much more of the produce from my garden.

The trick with drying is to do it fast enough that the food doesn't start to spoil during the process—and to keep it from re-hydrating afterwards from humidity in the air. I like to pack my dehydrated fruits and vegetables into Mason jars, twist the tops on tightly, and then store them out of direct light.

Electric dehydrators range from inexpensive round models to elaborate multi-tray supermodels that fit many cubic feet of produce at one time. That said, you should have a way to dry food off the grid if possible. I've built solar dehydrators that work well, albeit a lot slower than electric heat-and-fan-driven types. Pieces of window screening tacked to frames and set on a flat roof work well, provided the bugs and birds don't get to your produce. There are also plans online for small shed-style multi-tray solar dehydrators that are quite impressive.

Here in my climate the humidity and rain are very high during the harvest season, rendering solar dehydrating a big pain in the neck. There's nothing like waiting three days for some blueberries to dry, only to have a freak thunderstorm crash through and dump 4 inches of rain and ruin everything before you have a chance to run out the door and scoop up your drying produce.

Fermenting

Fermenting is a lot of fun, and it comes in two exciting and timeless styles: vinegar-forming and alcohol-forming.

Old-school pickle- and sauerkraut-making relied on the many bacteria in the air to turn vegetables in salt brine into pickled vegetables. The salt kept bad organisms from taking over while allowing the acid-forming ones to colonize the target. Yogurt contains many of the same microorganisms that are in live-fermented foods. If you've heard of acidophilus, that's one of the good guys. Live-fermented foods are really, really good for you and give your gut the ability to digest foods better as well as giving you greater health overall.

Unfortunately, we have replaced traditional fermentation with factory vinegar and sterile jars. If you buy pickles from the store, they're a dead food. Just vegetables sitting in a salty acid brine. If you make your own fermented foods, they are alive.

At its heart, it is putting vegetables into salt water and letting them sour up. However, there are a lot of different methods and traditions in fermenting that you'll want to explore on your own. I had my eyes opened on the value of live foods by reading the book *Wild Fermentation* by Sandor Katz. He's since written a much more authoritative book on the topic titled *The Art of Fermentation* with a lot of in-depth info, but *Wild Fermentation* is a great start for the first-time fermenter.

As a quick start into fermentation, here's how I make sauerkraut from our homegrown cabbages.

Easy Homemade Sauerkraut

First, grab a few cabbages, a food-grade bucket, a thrift-store plate that fits just inside the bucket, a towel, some non-iodized salt, and a knife.

1. Chop up the cabbage into smallish threads, and throw them in the bucket. Then add about a tablespoon of salt per each cabbage.

2. Smash the cabbage around with your fist, a pestle, a rock— or whatever—to bruise the chunks. Then put your plate on top of the shredded mess. The trick is to find a plate that almost fits your bucket diameter. You want to submerge the cabbage—and speaking of submerging, some recipes will tell you that the cabbage will make enough juice of its own when salted, which has never been the case for me.

3. Add water to cover the cabbage and the plate, throw in another tablespoon of salt, then put a weight on the plate to keep the cabbage pressed down beneath the brine. My favorite weight is a one-gallon wine bottle snagged from a recycling bin. Full of water, it's perfect.

4. Once your cabbage is all settled beneath the brine, the plate and the weight, place a towel over the whole thing to keep insects out. Tie it on with string or a bungee cable.

5. Wait a couple of weeks while checking every couple of days for scum or mold that may form on the surface of the brine. Skim it off—it won't hurt the kraut beneath. The bacteria in the air will do everything for you. The salt keeps spoilage microorganisms from taking hold, which clears the way

for vinegar-creating bacteria. That's right—you start with cabbage and salt and get vinegar brine. Pretty awesome.

Similar methods can be used to make dill pickles, kimchi, pickled onions, etc. It's not difficult, and the salt ensures that you're not going to make yourself sick with something like botulism. You may not have everything come out tasting great, but you're not going to poison yourself either, so long as the brine is nice and salty.

Now let's talk about alcohol fermentation. This is the really fun way to ferment and uses yeast rather than acid-forming bacteria.

Have you ever noticed how grapes have a white blush on their skin that you can rub off with your thumb? That's actually a thin layer of yeast. Yep, God designed grapes to ferment when crushed. When you get a couple of lusty maidens stomping them in a winepress, they immediately start transforming into something better than just grape juice. Interestingly, you can convert them to vinegar as well, simply by allowing more air into the fermentation process or by being less-than-careful in the wine-making process and introducing vinegar bacteria that beat out the yeast in the quest to consume the tasty grape sugars. I've heard it stated—and I believe it—that freshly pressed grape juice, untreated with chemicals, with not rot. It will either turn into wine or vinegar. What a great design. Crush grapes, and you get something good either way. And the live vinegar is also beneficial for your gut, unlike almost all store-bought vinegar.

But vinegar isn't what we want right now; we want alcohol. Here's how that happens.

When you have a sugary solution with the proper pH and introduce yeast, the yeast will rapidly start breeding and gobbling up the sugar while excreting alcohol. Eventually, the solution becomes so alcoholic that the yeast perish. At this point, it can be siphoned off, bottled, and set aside for continued oxidation to mellow the mix and broaden the flavor. Fresh wine or cider is usually pretty rough in flavor.

Quick story: when I was a young child I read about fermentation in a book I was reading on Louis Pasteur. This inspired me to get creative, so (without any kind of permission) I took some apple juice from the fridge, put it in a jar, and added some of mom's bread yeast from the refrigerator. It started bubbling along rapidly, and about a week later, I proclaimed to my younger brother and my friend Ray from down the street that I'd made beer and that I'd share it with them.

We snuck into my room with a few plastic cups from the pantry, and I poured out servings of the fizzy, strange-smelling apple juice "beer" for us to drink. I drank a little of mine and found it vile, but I tried to pretend I enjoyed it. My little brother (he was probably 5 years old at this point) tasted it, but I don't know if he finished his cup. Ray, however, drank his in little sips with much theatrics, proclaiming over and over again that it was "very good." He then told us he was drunk and pretended to fall over again and again, avoiding really drinking too much of the miserable stuff but proclaiming loudly that it was fantastic beer. After that less-than-satisfactory childhood experiment, I really didn't do much with fermentation again until I was out of the house and had piles of fruit to mess around with.

Making good wine or cider has thus far eluded me because I'm impatient. I'd rather make hard liquor, but that's illegal in the land of the free without a special license, so obviously I can't do it because it's impossible and have never done it and will never, ever, ever do it forever and ever until the laws change and suddenly make it a moral thing to do. At that point I'll get a huge copper still and put my mason jars to better use than just storing silly stuff like dried mushrooms and wild grape jam.

If, despite my impeccably upright stand on the issue, if you want to get serious and make liquor... it's not hard. I've heard from a friend that it's easier than making wine. If one were to take one's wife's pressure canner and do something like the setup in the diagram...

Yep, that would work. Distillation is just a matter of boiling the alcohol off and letting it re-condense without sending out too much water vapor at the same time. Hard liquor keeps indefinitely in bottles, unlike most wine, beer, and other lower-alcohol concoctions. It's also an incredible commodity. You can clean with alcohol, use it to power a motor, disinfect wounds, and even use it to take away guilt and feelings of worthlessness.

Though fruit alcohol is easy to produce, you can also make alcohol from grains and roots. This requires an extra step,

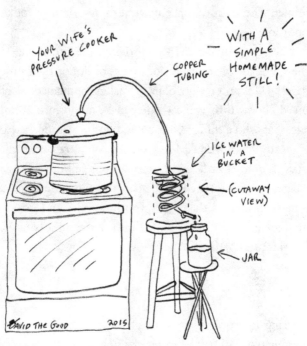

though, since yeasts aren't able to efficiently convert starches into alcohol. This is why grain is malted before fermentation.

Malting is simply a process of sprouting grains, then drying the very young sprouts. When, say, a kernel of corn geminates, an enzymatic process takes place that converts the stored starch into the kernel at least partially into simple sugars the emerging shoot can use for food. If you arrest this process directly as the seed starts to sprout, you can dry, grind, and ferment the grain to make magical things, such as vodka or bourbon.

The source materials, the distilling, the processing, and the aging are what give various types of liquor their unique flavors. This isn't really a book on making homemade alcohol, but do know this: you can safely make moonshine at home, and that whole thing about going blind if you do it wrong is mostly myth. You'd have to be a complete dunce to do that. The first little bit that comes out of your still when a batch of moonshine is made contains some methanol and other compounds that'll give you headaches and mess you up—tossing that first little bit of the run clears the batch. I've *heard* it's not hard at all.

Freezing

Freezing is the simplest form of preservation but requires freezing outdoor temperatures or a power source, meaning it may or may not be tenable in the apocalypse. If the power goes out for much more than a day or two, you'll lose your frozen food. Solar-powered chest freezers are a good idea if you decide to go the freezing route, especially since chest-style freezers are much more efficient than upright freezers and refrigerators. The cold air stays in, since it's heavier than the surrounding air.

Some fruits can be frozen directly; however, many vegetables deteriorate in the freezer unless they're first "blanched" to denature the enzymes that lead to decay. Blanching just means you heat up a big boiling pot of water, then throw your vegetables in it for a minute, then remove them and rapidly cool them in cold or icy water. To freeze them so they don't all stick together, you can then pat the vegetables dry with a towel and spread them out on a tray, then pop the tray in the freezer. When they're frozen solid an hour or two later, scrape them off the tray into well-sealed freezer bags or containers and pack them back into the freezer.

Vegetables taken directly from the garden that are then blanched and frozen retain most of their nutritional value. Frozen vegetables don't taste great forever, though, so I recommend eating them within a year for best flavor. We've done this with a surplus of collard greens and enjoyed them for almost a year. We've also frozen fresh peaches, mulberries, strawberries, blueberries, and bananas just by washing them and packing them into bags and had it work great. They are rather mushy when they thaw but work great for pies, jams, and smoothies. Next time you have an abundant harvest, don't let it go to waste. If you get too many apples, can apple butter, dry slices, make hard cider or applejack—or even chop and freeze some for pies.

Practice these food preservation techniques now, and there will be one less skill you'll have to learn in an emergency.

Chapter 9

Conclusion

Knowing how to grow your own food is one of the greatest skills you can learn, and it's one of the best lessons you can pass on to your children.

Pulling a homegrown carrot from the warm earth or grinding your own cornmeal connects you to traditions that have endured through a million crises, both national and personal. If you can farm, you greatly reduce the likelihood that you'll go hungry.

Start buying good tools. Start making compost. Start a little garden and then a big garden and then a huge garden. Save seeds when you can. Preserve what you grow. Thank God for every opportunity to put your hands in the soil and take part in the miracle of gardening.

A stock market crash or a faraway terrorist attack doesn't mean as much when you're looking at thousands of calories of potatoes or a tree loaded with fruit. Sometimes it's best to shrug and walk away from the madness. Spending time in the garden growing your own food will make you into a better person and teach you the skills you need to survive.

If you have questions or are looking for more inspiration, go to my website www.thesurvivalgardener.com and read my archive of posts. I also invite you to sign up for The Survival Gardening Newsletter while you're there so you'll get more gardening inspiration delivered to your inbox.

Thank you for reading. I hope I've inspired to you get outside and get planting. May you have great success no matter what happens in this crazy world, and may your thumbs always be green.

Appendix 1:
The Emergency
Quick-Start Guide

If you just picked up this book post-Event in the charred rubble of your prepper neighbor's house while looking for food, then—hi, I'm David The Good, and I'm going to tell you what to do right away to start a survival garden.

I assume you'll be starting your garden on that most ridiculous of American frivolities, a lawn.

Note: Before you do anything on this list, I highly recommend you repent of your sins, ask God for forgiveness and mercy, then pray He'll give you favor. Without Providence on your side, all your hard work will fail.

And don't forget to double-tap the zombies!

1. Prepare Your Space

If it's spring, summer, or early fall, mark off a big space—at least 4,000 square feet, if possible (that's a 40- by 100-foot garden), then till the area under. If you don't have access to a tiller or a tractor, you'll need to fork or dig to loosen the area and remove the grass. There's more on that in Chapter 1. I hope you have at least a shovel.

Once you've turned the soil, water the area well, if possible, to cause the weeds to germinate. Pick out any clumps of grass. A landscaping rake is useful for this if you can find one. If you're using a tiller, wait a week after the initial tilling, then till again to kill the emerging weeds and returning grass. If you've dug by hand and picked out the weeds as you went, skip waiting the week, and start planting.

2. Hunt for Seeds

Now hunt for seeds. Read Appendix 2 on planting from a pantry for ideas. If you can't find anything to plant whatsoever, you'd better start learning to eat beetlegrubs and snakes.

3. Hunt for Fertilizer

It's time to start saving your urine. Do it. Tell the rest of your comrades, if any have survived, to save theirs as well. This will be your fertilizer; do not waste it. Also look for any bags of fertilizer, compost, or lime you can scavenge. Hunt for manure, and start composting your own (if you can find a copy of my other book *Compost Everything*, it tells you how to do this safely. If you can't fid it, that's fine. Just bury your waste beneath the soil and plant on it the next season).

4. Start Planting

Rake your plot to create a fine seedbed, then create rows. Though I would normally plant a lot of seeds and thin out, if your seed supply is limited, do not do this. Plant every seed carefully, and give them enough space to fend for themselves if rainfall is low. Water the rows after planting.

5. Find a Hoe

Once you've done this, look for any kind of hoe. If you can't find one, make one from whatever you can find. A flat stone lashed to a well-proportioned branch can work. A piece of metal is better. The idea is to get an edge that can slide just under the ground and decapitate weeds. You're going to need a hoe to control weeds.

6. Start Fertilizing

Once your seedlings emerge, sprinkle a little fertilizer alongside each one, or thin out your collected urine to 6–10 parts water to one part urine, and water each seedling carefully with the mix. Urine is high in nitrogen and contains a wide range of other nutrients your body is unable to use and therefore excretes. It's also safe to use in the garden.

7. Maintain the Plot

Spend at least a portion of every day in the garden. This isn't a hobby any more—it's your life. Pick off insects, carefully weed around every crop, keep the grass from creeping in from the outside, and be sure to fertilize with diluted urine every two weeks.

8. Set Aside Some Plants for Seed

Since seeds may not be available for purchase during a crisis, make sure you leave about 15 percent of your plants as seed plants for the next crop. Some crops have portions that can be eaten without losing the seeds, such as winter squash, tomatoes, and leaf lettuce. With other crops such as beans and peas, you can't have your seeds and eat them too. Be sure to save seeds from as many plants as possible to lower the problems associated with inbreeding. This doesn't matter much with beans and winter squash; however, corn is very susceptible to inbreeding, so you need to make sure you save some kernels from at least 100 plants—although 200 is much better—or your yields will rapidly plummet year-after-year. Dry your seeds well, and pack them away in scavenged jars for next year's garden, provided there is a next year.

9. Store the Harvest

Dry, ferment, freeze, root cellar, can your produce, and ration carefully. Keep out beetles, mice, moths, and other vermin as best as you can, or they will eat your produce before you can. If you don't have a root cellar yet, dig one.

10. Harvest and Replant

If you started in spring or summer, you may have enough time left to plant again for a fall or even a winter crop, depending on your climate. Do this if possible, concentrating on roots and highly nutritious greens such as kale. Malnutrition will screw you up. Greens may not be filling, but they will keep you healthy. Roots will keep you running. If you don't have enough year left to plant for fall, prepare for next year by keeping weeds from going to seed and by trenching compost, manure, and other amendments into your garden space over the winter (unless the ground is frozen solid—then just make a compost pile convenient to the garden). Increase the size of your garden if possible by continuing to double-dig new areas. Don't give up!

A quick guide follows as to what can be planted when. More information on these crops is provided in Chapter 7.

Crops to Plant in Late Spring or Summer

- Amaranth
- Beans
- Buckwheat
- Cassava
- Chaya
- Corn
- Cucumbers
- Eggplant
- Ginger (tropical—can also be planted in fall and winter)

- Melons
- Moringa
- Okra
- Peppers
- Squash and Pumpkin
- Sweet Potatoes
- Tobacco
- Tomatoes
- Tree Collards (can be planted year-round)
- Yams (tropical climate required except for Chinese yam)
- Zucchini

Crops to Plant in Late Winter/Early Spring/Fall)

- Barley
- Beets
- Broccoli
- Brussels Sprouts
- Cabbage
- Carrots
- Cauliflower
- Collards
- Fava Beans
- Garlic
- Jerusalem artichokes (tubers must be planted in winter or spring)
- Kale
- Kohlrabi

- Lettuce
- Mustard
- Onions
- Peas
- Potatoes
- Radishes
- Rye
- Spinach
- Sugarcane (tropical—doesn't like frost—plant canes in fall)
- Tree Collards (can be planted year-round)
- Turnips
- Wheat
- Yams (tropical climate required except for Chinese yam)

Appendix 2: A Survival Garden From Your Pantry

I discovered in kindergarten that you could plant a bean seed, and it would grow. At age six, heady with this knowledge and drunk with power, I raided my mom's pantry, and planted a significant number of her dry beans any place I could find some open ground or an abandoned pot.

It's only gotten worse from there. I'm decades older and I am still a seed fiend. A couple of years ago I realized how serious this problem was when my wife and I were at a party one evening, and I was watching the hostess make guacamole.

In horror, I saw her pitch an avocado pit into the trash.

Me: "You can grow that!" I said.

Hostess: "Oh yeah?" (not interested).

Me: "Yes! In fact, if you're not going to plant it, I am!"

With that, I dug around in the trashcan until I found it, then carefully wrapped it in a napkin and stuffed the pit into the pocket of my jeans.

The hostess raised an eyebrow, but I ignored her. After all, *she* was a murderer! It wasn't *me* that was weird! *She* was the one tossing a poor defenseless embryo in the trash! It was like a plant abortion!

My gosh, just thinking about it makes me sick. "What has this world come to?"

When I explained this reasoning to my wife, she recommended I calm down and maybe get some counseling.

Wife: "You know, avocados don't even grow in our climate. What are you going to do with it?

Me: "I'll plant it in a pot, then give it to someone farther south. Or just keep it in a pot. I want my own avocados, dang it!"

Wife: "You can't save them all, you know."

Me: "Did Schindler say that?"

Wife: "You know what? You're nuts. Just calm down and have a Martini or something. Maybe I can pop some popcorn?"

Me: *"Murderer!"*

Anyhow, my wife's misunderstanding and bloodthirstiness (sapthirstiness?) aside, have you ever considered how you'd deal with a collapse in shipping or any number of things that might cause a total breakdown of the supply lines?

Like... if you couldn't get seeds for some crazy reason, or you've bugged out to the country and forgotten your filing cabinet of heirloom varieties—what would you do?

Could you plant a garden?

The answer, most likely, is yes. You just have to think a little differently. Here's a quick look at what you can grow just by digging through the burnt-out remains of a grocery store... or the pantry of an average home.

Corn

Corn is a great staple as I've covered back in Chapter 7... and almost everyone has some popcorn sitting around somewhere. Someone might say, "Great, Dave. You're telling me I'm gonna plant popcorn during the apocalypse?"

Don't knock it.

Popcorn can be used for flour, which can be used for cornbread, grits, etc. It can also feed chickens. Even better? Popcorn is not yet a genetically modified corn, so you can grow it and save seeds without worrying if you're going to get tumors or something. It's an excellent grain. This would be a top pick if I was looting. Call me the Orville Redenbacher of the Apocalypse—I'll be watching it all, popcorn in hand. It's bound to be entertaining.

Beans and their kin

And hey... look at that! Protein! Believe it or not, most dried beans will sprout if you plant them. They also grow fast, so in a relatively short time after planting, you'll have many times the number of beans you started with. Some, like navy beans, are even good as green beans. Since beans are a nitrogen fixer, I often buy bags of them for a buck or two, then scatter them across broken ground a few months before I plant other crops.

In the winter, I plant dry peas, chickpeas, lentils, and fava beans. Most of these are available in the pantry.

Melons, eggplants, winter squash, and tomatoes

Though you might not find these in the pantry, you can often find them in dumpsters. When you plant their seeds, you may not get an awesome variety since many commercial varieties are hybrids. That said, you will still get something to grow and eat when you plant their seeds. My aunt once dropped a slice of tomato from a burger she was eating in the garden and a short time later, there was a little ring of tomato sprouts there. Take care of those little sprouts, and a few months later you'll be eating tomatoes. I've done it many times, mostly because we compost everything that comes through the house and I'm a sucker for the volunteer plants that pop up.

Potatoes and sweet potatoes

"Don't plant potatoes from the store! They've been sprayed with sprout inhibitors! They may carry potato blight!" Yeah, yeah, yeah. I know. I've heard that. And sure, it's good to get certified virus-free seed when you plant white potatoes, but we're talking collapse gardening here, not ideal gardening. If a potato has eyes on it, it's likely going to grow. I've stuffed forgotten store-bought potatoes in the ground many times and had success. Sweet potatoes are even easier to deal with. Just one potato in the corner of your pantry can produce a lot of slips for your garden—and feed you many pounds of tubers by fall.

Birdseed

"Birdseed? Your wife is right! You're nuts!"

No, seriously. What's in birdseed? Sunflower seed, millet, sorghum, corn, peanuts (more common in "squirrel feed")— it depends on the variety, but many of the seeds birds eat are also good for people to eat. If your adorable parakeet dies during the initial shockwave, once the radiation in the backyard goes down a little you can plant a nice garden in his memory.

Ginger, garlic, and onions

Is there some ginger root in your fridge? A few onions? A head of garlic on the counter? All of these can be planted. An onion will grow leaves that can be harvested like chives – and if you're lucky, it will later go to seed and provide you with another generation of onions. Individual cloves of garlic can be planted in the fall or spring (depending on your climate) and grown into entire heads of garlic. Ginger can be put in a big pot if you're north of USDA zone 9—just bring the pot in during winter. It will grow and spread into a plant that has not only culinary but medicinal uses. (Nothing calms a queasy stomach like ginger!)

Herb seeds

Beyond the basic crops in the pantry and fridge, you can also check your spice cabinet for further gardening loot. Dill, coriander, and mustard seed are common seasonings that are also worth growing. Bonus: coriander is the seed of the cilantro plant. That means if you find some seeds, you can experiment with tasty post-apocalyptic salsa recipes. My favorite so far is my Grandma's classic "Million-rad Chili Dipper." We used to put that on our vault rations when I was a kid.

At least, we wanted to. Our tomato crop failed most years thanks to the firedamp, rendering salsa impossible.

Random goodies

If you're lucky, you might come across someone who likes making bread from scratch. A gallon of wheat berries can plant a big plot of grain. If you're related to health-food nuts or someone who is gluten intolerant, you could also come across quinoa, amaranth, and other small pseudo-grains. Feed stores carry big bags of oats, corn, and other strange things, so if everything collapses, go there. If they're already closed, look for someone who owns horses or chickens, and beg a few handfuls of seed.

The point is this: seeds, roots, and other planting materials are everywhere. It makes a lot of sense to stock up on really good seeds ahead of time—but if you miss that window, all is not lost.